MW01612009

What othe
Raising An Earth Friendly Child

"A lively, sensible, and practical guide . . . differs from its popular predecessor, the Earthworks Group's '50 Simple Things Kids Can Do To Save The Earth' in that these activities are designed for parents and children to do together, thereby promoting adult awareness and family values as well."

--Library Journal

*"Put **Raising An Earth Friendly Child** next to the crib . . . parents who are aware of today's environmental problems will want to be ready when their children are. This source of information and ideas will help prepare children for the challenge of saving the planet."*

--Lester Brown, President
Worldwatch Institute

"Holds a wealth of ideas to teach children about saving their environment . . . designed in an easy-to-follow format."
--The Cedar Rapids Gazette

*"A very important guide for the future citizens of the planet to help them develop a caring and healthy attitude toward the environment. This book should **indeed** be on every parent's bookshelf."*

--Actress Donna Mills

Raising an Earth Friendly Child

The Keys to Your Child's Happy, Healthy Future

Level I

by
Debbie J. Tilsworth

Raising an Earth Friendly Child

The Keys to Your Child's Happy, Healthy Future

by Debbie J. Tilsworth

THIS BOOK IS PRINTED ON RECYCLED PAPER

Published by:

Raven Press
1900 Raven Drive
Fairbanks, Alaska 99709-8358 U.S.A.

Cover Design and Illustration: Karen Stomberg
Book Design: Jill Marshall, Marshall Arts
Editor: Timothy Tilsworth, Ph.D., Professor of Environmental
Engineering, University of Alaska Fairbanks

First Printing 1991
Second Printing 1991

Library of Congress Catalog Number 90-91931
Tilsworth, Debbie J.
Raising an Earth Friendly Child: The Keys to Your Child's
Happy, Healthy Future / Level I

ISBN 0-9627446-7-0 $19.95 Softcover

For Craig and Pat

Acknowledgements

I am indebted to my husband Tim for his assistance with this project. His editorial guidance and expertise have been invaluable. I owe much to his interest in the environment and his many contributions to the project. Without his support, this book would not have been written.

I am also grateful for Jill Marshall's talent and professionalism. Her genius for design improved the format and appearance of this book considerably, and I appreciate the many touches she added throughout.

I wish to thank Karen Stomberg of Great Northern Design Works for illustrating the cover of this book. She spent many extra hours on the project, and Tim and I appreciate her commitment to achieving the effect we desired.

Finally, I am grateful to my parents, Don and Ruth May. They taught us the value of reaching for our dreams, setting goals, and working hard. For their love and encouragement, I will always be grateful.

Table of Contents

INTRODUCTION

Welcome! You are about to start a journey that will lead you and your child to a happier, healthier future. Some of you are farther along this path than others. However, it doesn't matter where you start, just so long as you start.

This book is a collection of activities for you and your child to do together. You don't need any special training to teach the skills in this book—just the ability to follow simple guidelines.

The activities are easy and fun. Be as creative with them as you wish, and feel free to adapt them to your child's talents. Each section includes a suggested age range and a list of materials needed. In almost every case the materials are readily available in your home. You won't have to spend additional money. *Your only investment is time.*

And that brings us to the next point. With so many single-parent families and families where both parents work outside the home, time is scarce. There are too many things to do and too little time to do them.

Sound familiar?

It's a reality for most of us. But think about it: is an hour each week too much to invest in teaching your child the skills he needs to be happy and healthy in the 21st century?

You know the dangers: global warming, acid rain, the green-house effect, polluted rivers and oceans, ground water depletion, overpopulation, closed landfills, air pollution. The 1990s are our last chance to reverse the trends that have the potential to destroy our earth. After that it may be too late.

Protecting the environment is no longer a luxury. *It's a matter of survival.* And you have already put too much love and energy into raising your child to ignore this crucial fact.

Because children learn best by doing, the discovery approach is used in most activities. This engages your child's interest and gets him involved in discovering solutions to problems. It's much more effective than simply telling him what to do.

You are the best judge of your child's abilities. While an age range of 6 - 10 years may be suggested for an activity, your 5 year old may be quite capable of doing it. Please feel free to tailor each activity to your child's development.

The importance of your participation cannot be over-emphasized. *As the parent or primary caretaker, your example is the most critical part of this process.* If you make protecting the environment a priority, so will your child. And by doing these activities together, you not only keep each other on the right track, but you also enhance your relationship.

There are 52 chapters in this book. It's not necessary to follow them in order, especially since some are seasonal in nature. If possible, try one chapter a week. Set aside an hour or two every weekend for an earth friendly activity (if that's the most convenient time), and make it a date with your child. It's an excellent way to spend quality time together.

At the end of the book we have included a Question & Answer section in case you or your child have questions about the environment. Please refer to it whenever you wish.

Don't be discouraged if you can't change some habits overnight. The first step is awareness. After that you may wish to phase in new practices over time. Remember that some alternatives may be better in the short run but worse in the long run, or vice versa. Before you make changes, it's a good idea to consider their long and short term effects.

As you know, children tend to see the world in black and white terms. When you introduce a new concept, they may be quick to judge old habits as "bad." Explain that it takes time to change, especially when you're used to doing things a certain way. But don't be afraid to let your child's conscience influence you. It can be very effective for both of you as you become more earth friendly.

The important thing to remember is that every little bit helps. Some of you will choose not to take all of the steps mentioned in this book. But the steps you do take will make a difference. With 250 million people in the United States and 5 billion worldwide, little steps multiply to big results.

Our goal is to encourage you and your child to live in harmony with the environment. We have tried to be objective in presenting what we believe are earth friendly practices. However, we realize that some people may not agree with all the ideas in this book. For example, some trappers use methods to trap animals that they consider to be earth friendly. We don't condone trapping animals for fur, but we recognize that some trappers try to be more humane than others.

We hope that you will take pleasure in teaching your child earth friendly skills. With your help, he can have a happy, healthy future.

Please write to let us know about your progress. We're interested in finding out how the activities work for you and your child.

Thanks — and HAVE FUN!

Debbie Tilsworth
c/o RAVEN PRESS
1900 Raven Drive, Suite 101
Fairbanks, Alaska 99709-8358

WHAT IS THE ENVIRONMENT?

Is it the birds and the bees? The flowers and the trees?

Yes, and much more. The environment consists of the animals, plants, water, air and land around us. Everything has its own special way of relating to the rest of the world. If we disrupt one thing, it impacts other things too.

Some things are more friendly to people than others. For example, we may think of bees as unfriendly because they sting. But flowers are dependent upon bees to pollinate them, and most of us enjoy flowers. Whether something is friendly or unfriendly sort of depends on our perspective, doesn't it? To flowers, bees are friendly.

Everything has a place and a purpose. We're all part of the environment, and the better we understand it the easier it will be to live in harmony with the earth.

Let's review a few basics before you and your child begin the activities:

Water

We can't live without it. We drink it, cook with it, bathe in it, sprinkle it on our lawn, wash our clothes in it, and flush our waste with it.

All our fresh water comes from the atmosphere or the ground. When ground water is used faster than it is replaced, the water table falls. And if you live by the ocean, sea water may seep in. Ground water can also be polluted by people who spill oil, gasoline, sewage or other substances on the ground.

Water continuously travels through a cycle. As it evaporates from the earth, it forms water vapor. The vapor rises until it reaches cold air, condenses, and turns into clouds. Then it rains, and the cycle begins again.

This cycle is driven by the sun's heat energy. It causes the water in every body of water to be replaced, some more quickly than others. For example, the water in a river is replaced every 10 to 20 days, but a deep lake may take 100 years.

When toxic chemicals filter down into the ground water, they may pollute an enormous amount of water. Pollution from just one factory may contaminate the water in several cities.

Most polluted water runs off the surface of the ground and into streams, lakes and rivers. From there it flows into the ocean. And the oceans are not big enough to absorb all the waste that people discharge into them.

Shortages of fresh water exist in many areas of the United States. Since water use has grown faster than our population, water shortages are getting worse.

The best way to increase the fresh water supply is to conserve our use of it. And the best way to keep water fresh is to prevent pollutants from entering the soil.

Land

We need land to grow food, build houses, and produce minerals such as gold, silver and copper. Most of us spend our entire life on land.

Nearly all the energy on the earth's surface comes from the sun. Solar energy warms the earth, evaporates water, and creates wind. It is responsible for our weather.

Life on earth requires a few essentials: a moderate temperature, energy, water, soil, and air. Given these few essentials, there are millions of species that share the earth with us.

Biologists estimate there are 5 million species; but they expect that one-fifth of all species (about 1 million) will become extinct by the end of the 20th century.

Why?

Because people are destroying their habitat.

A habitat is the physical area where an organism lives. Two factors control the kind of plants that can live in a habitat: temperature and rainfall. In places that receive a lot of rain, you can expect to find large trees. And places with lighter rainfall may only have small trees or shrubs. The plants in a habitat determine which other organisms can grow there too.

In addition, plants release oxygen into the air for us to breathe. The carbon dioxide that we exhale is used by plants. It's the perfect complement to human life.

To protect the diversity of life on earth, we must stop destroying the habitat of species.

Air

We need air to breathe so that we can take oxygen from the air into our lungs, and then to our bloodstream. We use such large amounts of air that it cannot have many contaminants in it. Once air is polluted, it is very difficult to clean.There are two main problems associated with air that will affect the entire world. They are ozone depletion and the greenhouse effect.

We are destroying the earth's ozone layer, which is formed from oxygen and energy from the sun. It is a protective barrier that screens out most ultraviolet rays. As you know, ultraviolet rays cause skin cancer and kill many other organisms outright.

In the 1980s scientists discovered the large, growing hole in the ozone layer over Antarctica. If unchecked, this hole could expand until it threatens our existence.

Damage to the ozone layer comes mainly from chlorofluoro-carbons, known as CFCs. CFCs are used in aerosol sprays, refrigerators, and air conditioners. Once released into the air, CFCs float into the atmosphere and break down the ozone layer.

Imagine the year 2050. Summers are 10 degrees warmer than today. The homes of 20 million people on the East Coast are under water. The Rocky Mountains are no longer covered with snow. The farmlands of the United States have turned into a dry dust bowl because there is no rain during the growing season. Why? The greenhouse effect has set in.

The greenhouse effect is the increasing temperature of the earth, brought about by gases that are trapped in the atmosphere. The two main culprits are methane and carbon dioxide.

Methane is generated by materials that decay without oxygen, and by the world's grazing animals: cows, sheep, goats, and water buffalo. The expansion of agriculture is largely responsible for more methane in the air.

But carbon dioxide is a far worse enemy. It comes from burning fossil fuels such as coal, oil, gasoline, and natural gas. Every time we burn wood we release carbon dioxide into the air. And since people exhale carbon dioxide, the more people there are, the worse the problem gets.

Just when we're putting more carbon dioxide than ever into the air, we're also cutting down more trees—the very things that use it up.

Our Challenge

Our challenge is to understand how we are hurting the earth, and to stop it.

One way you can help is to make sure your child learns to be earth friendly. It's more than an attitude, although it certainly starts there. It's the willingness to act in a way that is friendly to the environment.

Things weren't perfect when we were born. But we can leave them better than when we found them.

Remember: the environment is the birds and the bees, and the flowers and the trees, and everything around us.

Our children deserve to inherit it in healthy condition, don't you think?

SHOWER SCROOGE

Background

The earth's supply of fresh water is being used much faster than it is being replaced. Most of us use more water than we realize, and nearly half of the water we use in our homes is in the bathroom—for showers, baths, shaving, brushing teeth, and flushing the toilet.

At a convenient time, explain to your child that the earth may run out of fresh water unless we take steps to conserve it. The fresh water beneath the ground is called ground water, and it took many thousands of years to get there. Now that so many people are using so much water, there are areas in the United States with shortages.

Ask your child if he can guess how much water he uses for his daily showers. Let him write his guess on a piece of paper and put it in a safe place. Then ask him to time the length of his next shower, so that he can see how much water he actually used.

The Goal

To reduce the amount of water used in your child's shower by 50%. (Note: taking half as many showers is not an option.)

Age Range

5 - 10 years

Materials Needed

Stopwatch, paper and pen, masking tape.

❖

ACTIVITY 1

Your child should start the stopwatch when he turns on the water for his shower and stop it as soon as he turns off the faucet. After he's dressed, ask him how long it took. Round off the seconds to the nearest minute. Then help him multiply each minute by 5 gallons to give him the approximate amount of water he used. (For example, if his shower lasted 5 minutes, you would multiply that by 5 and get 25 gallons of water.)

Let your child write the answer on a sheet of paper and compare it to his earlier guess. How close was he?

If he's old enough, ask him to figure out how much water he uses to shower in an average week, month, and year. Ask him for ideas to reduce this amount.

Some ideas include:

- Use tap water to soap up his body before turning on the shower

- Don't turn on the water at full force

- Use only enough water to rinse off

- Help Mom or Dad install a low-flow shower head that cuts the flow to 3 gallons a minute or less

ACTIVITY 2

Riddle: Which uses less water, a shower or a bath? To find out, have your child take a bath one morning and a shower the next. Use the masking tape. Write: "Kevin's bath" and stick it on the inside of the tub at the water level before he drains it.

When he takes a shower, have him plug the drain so that the water is caught in the tub. After he's finished showering, label another piece of tape "Kevin's shower" and stick it at the water level. Time how long the water runs for each activity.

Did the shower or the bath use less water? Ask your child to draw conclusions. If there are savings involved, see if he can calculate them. (Use the standard 1 minute = 5 gallons).

ACTIVITY 3

Shower Scrooge. If you have one child, make this a two or three-way competition between him and you, the parent(s). Or make it a competition between your children. The object is to see which of you can use the least amount of water for a shower and still get clean.

Plug the drain for your shower. Afterwards, mark the water level with masking tape, noting your name and the date. See which of you can get the lowest mark in a week's time. The winner is CHAMPION SHOWER SCROOGE.

If you suspect your child of cutting corners on cleanliness, insist on a simple inspection. Let him examine your ears or toes, if you wish. That'll show him you're being fair with the contest. And of course, the reward for winning is up to you. Make it something that motivates your child, but keep it simple and inexpensive—like a back rub or bedtime story.

Note: Activities 2 and 3 assume that you can take showers in your bathtub. Please don't try them if you only have a shower stall in your house.

TOOTH-WASTE BUSTERS

Background

Another way to conserve water in our homes is to be more careful when we brush our teeth. At first it may not seem like we waste much water by letting it run as we brush our teeth, but it's surprising how much goes down the drain in a few minutes.

Now that your child knows how much she uses in an average shower, ask her to guess how much water is wasted while she brushes her teeth. Ask her to write her guess on a piece of paper and put it in a safe place. If she isn't sure how to estimate it, show her some measuring cups and a quart, half gallon and/or gallon containers. That should assist her as she makes her guess.

Let her know that you'd like her to find out how much water she actually uses to brush her teeth that evening before she goes to bed. Or let her choose the morning, whichever time is more convenient for both of you.

The Goal

To reduce the amount of water wasted while your child brushes her teeth (or washes her face) by 75% or more.

Age Range

4 - 10 years

Materials Needed

Toothbrush, toothpaste and several sizes of containers (1 quart, half gallon, gallon), paper and pen.

ACTIVITY 1

Place an appropriate size container under the faucet so that it can collect water. Ask your child to brush her teeth as she does normally. (It doesn't matter if she spits into the container.) You may need to assist her by placing other containers under the faucet as they fill up. When she is through, remove the containers and take them into the kitchen. Pour them into the gallon size container.

• How much water did she use? Was it a gallon or more?

• If your child uses this much water twice a day to brush her teeth, how much will she use in a day? A week? A month? A year? Help her figure out the answers.

Talk to her about how she can become a "Tooth-Waste Buster" by using these tricks:

• Wet the toothbrush first and turn off the faucet. Put toothpaste on the brush. Brush teeth thoroughly before turning on the water again.

• Never leave the water running while brushing teeth.

ACTIVITY 2

Now ask your child to brush her teeth again. Use a container to measure how much *less* water she needs. Help her calculate the water savings.

Incentives: Post a chart with your child's name on it next to the sink. For each day she is a "Tooth-Waste Buster" let her put a star by her name. See how many stars she can collect. Stickers or checkmarks work equally well. Be sure to praise her for her efforts.

Variations: The same activity applies to washing your child's face ("Face-Waster"). Get her to collect water in a container while she washes her face in the evening. See how much she uses with the water running continuously. Compare it to the savings when she shuts off the faucet after wetting her washcloth and using water only for quick rinses of the washcloth. You'll both be amazed at the difference.

Tip: Learning by example is one of the best ways to teach your child. Don't let her catch you being a Tooth-Waster or a Face-Waster!

COLOR-CODED RECYCLABLES

Background

Currently 90% of our trash is dumped in landfill sites and buried. These dumps are filling up fast, and over a third of them have been closed since 1980. People are reluctant to allow new landfills to be opened near their homes because they are afraid of ground water or air pollution. Landfills nearby would also decrease their property values.

The best way to begin tackling the trash problem is to recycle your family's newspapers, glass and aluminum cans. Every product that can be recycled saves room at the landfill, and it also conserves our natural resources.

Ask your child if he knows what happens when he throws out trash. He may think only as far as the large disposal bags or the dump truck. Explain that most trash ends up buried in the earth, and the earth is getting too full to take much more.

The Goal

To teach your child to separate newspapers, glass and aluminum cans from other garbage for recycling.

Age Range

2 - 5 years

Materials Needed

Four different colors of waste cans, a box, a picture of an aluminum can (clipped from a magazine), pictures of glass containers (clear, green and brown), scotch tape, several aluminum cans and glass containers, a newspaper.

❖

ACTIVITY 1

Code the waste cans. Assist your child to tape the picture of the aluminum can on the side or top of the first waste can; tape the picture of a clear glass container on the second waste can; and the green and brown glass pictures on the other two waste cans. Set the box nearby for newspapers.

ACTIVITY 2

Hand your child a green glass bottle and ask him to throw it out. Praise him when he deposits it in the correct container. Try other colors of glass bottles, the newspaper, and several aluminum cans. Have fun with the game. Trade places and let him test you. Deposit one incorrectly and see if he "catches" you.

ACTIVITY 3

When the containers are full, ask your child to help you cart the separated items to the recycling center. (Check for specific sites in your community—they may be at a supermarket, shopping mall, or commercial recycling center.) Make the excursion pleasant. Perhaps you could stop for a treat afterwards, or eat breakfast at a restaurant if it's on a weekend.

Hint: Try to instill a sense of satisfaction in your child for helping recycle these goods. Any positive comments you make will be long remembered.

4

SHOPPING
BOO-BOOS

Background

The way most of us shop is not very friendly to the environment. We waste energy getting to the store, we allow our goods to be bagged in throw-away plastic or paper, and we choose far too many disposable items.

Before you go to the store some weekend, talk to your child about some shopping "smart cuts" (as opposed to "short cuts"). Discuss the following smart cuts:

- Paper bags are made from trees. If we use cloth bags or reuse the same paper bags on each trip to the store, we could save the life of one tree each year.

- Whenever possible, buy products in glass or aluminum containers. They're easier to recycle than other items.

- Avoid all products packaged in styrofoam. It lasts up to 500 years in landfills and contributes to the greenhouse effect.

- Throw-away items like paper plates and plastic forks clog up landfills. Whenever possible, it's better to use washable dishes.

- Buy as many fresh products as you can. They are usually more nutritious and it cuts down on packaging.

- Don't buy products with too much packaging, such as those with individually wrapped portions.

- Look for packaging that has "Recycled" or "Recyclable" on it.

- Avoid products that contain CFCs, such as aerosol sprays.

- Use natural alternatives to cleaning products whenever

possible. Some good choices are baking soda and vinegar.

- Driving to the store uses gasoline. This also contributes to the greenhouse effect. The less we drive our automobiles the better.

Explain to your child that a "Shopping Boo-Boo" is when you buy something that doesn't pay attention to these smart cuts. For example, a "Shopping Boo-Boo" might be buying plastic plates or aerosol sprays, or forgetting to take paper bags to the store with you.

The Goal
To reduce the number of "Shopping Boo-Boos" you and your child make when selecting goods at the store.

Age Range
6 - 10 years

Materials Needed
Bicycles, reusable shopping bags (cloth or paper), pad of paper and pen.

ACTIVITY 1

Peddle Power. Is the nearest store within bicycle distance? If so, it's great exercise, a fun family activity, and good for the environment. Attach a receptacle to your bike or take a backpack. And be sure to bring along cloth bags or paper bags. You're off to a wonderful start!

ACTIVITY 2

Ask your child to use her pad of paper and pen and silently follow you around. Every time she sees you commit a "Shopping Boo-Boo," she should make a mark on her paper and write (or draw) what the "Boo-Boo" was. As you go through the aisles, have fun with her. Pretend to consider a package of paper plates and put them in your cart. Then, when you see her start to make a note on her pad, "catch" yourself and put it back. When you get home, talk about how many "Boo-Boos" she discovered. See if there are any alternatives, and discuss what you could do differently next time. Keep track of the number of "Boo-Boos" per trip, and watch them decline.

ACTIVITY 3

On a subsequent trip, let your child pick out items. Tell her what you need, ask her what she thinks is the most earth friendly selection, and let her put it in your cart. This will develop her critical thinking abilities, and it will also reinforce good choices.

5

POPULATION PUZZLE

Background

The earth's population, already around 5 billion people, is estimated to be between 6 and 7 billion by the year 2000. This increase in the number of people will deplete our supply of water, wood and fossil fuels. Because the size of our population is at the root of most of our problems, one of our most important challenges is to control it.

Explain to your child that one of the difficulties with having too many people on earth is that there aren't enough resources to go around. It means that there is less food, water, land and energy for everyone. Life becomes less enjoyable when people have to compete for resources. To maintain a high quality of life, we need to keep our population from growing too fast.

Ask your child to guess how many people there would be over a 100 year period if one person had four children, and each of his children had four children, etc. Let him write his guess on a piece of paper, but don't let him figure it out. After he's written down his guess, ask him to try an experiment to see how many people result from different sizes of families.

The Goal

To lead your child to the discovery of how many people result from families of 1 or more children within a 100-year period.

Age Range:

6 - 10 years

Materials Needed

Box of toothpicks, kitchen table, paper and pencil.

ACTIVITY 1

Let your child arrange one toothpick at the top of your table, representing one person. For the first activity, assume that the person has one child. Let him place a toothpick directly beneath it to represent that child. Assume that the child grows up and has one child. Place a toothpick directly beneath it to indicate that child. Go through five (5) generations. After the fifth generation, subtract the first toothpick to allow for deaths. How many people (toothpicks) did your child start with? How many did he end up with? Write down the number.

ACTIVITY 2

Let your child arrange one toothpick at the top of your table, again representing a person. Now assume that this person has two children, and each of those two children has two more children. Your child should arrange the toothpicks accordingly. After five generations, he needs to subtract the first toothpick. How many people (toothpicks) does he end up with? Write the number on a piece of paper.

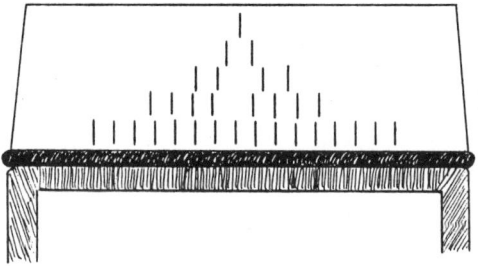

ACTIVITY 3

Do the same exercise, except assume that each person has three children. How many people does your child end up with? Note the results on a piece of paper.

ACTIVITY 4

Assume four children for each person. How many people does your child end up with? Again, note the results.

ACTIVITY 5

(Optional) Assume five or six children for each person. How many people does your child end up with?

Discuss the implications of this exercise with your child. Compare his results of the four-child family with his earlier guess. He should be able to tell from the large number of toothpicks at the bottom of the table how rapidly people multiply in a 100 year period. Compare the results of a one-child family with a four-child family.

Ask your child what he thinks the ideal solution might be. Does he mention limiting the size of families to 1 or 2 children? If so, he's right on track.

6

EARTH BANK:
The Game

Background

Our earth started out millions of years ago with enough water, trees, air and sunlight to sustain life. Now, with our population at 5 billion people, we are in danger of using up our resources.

Explain to your child that the earth is like a bank. Deposits are made in the form of sunlight, rain, and oxygen-producing trees. Withdrawals are made by people who use water, energy, or products that deplete the earth's resources.

The more withdrawals there are, the fewer deposits (or resources) remain in the bank. Unless we are able to find a balance, the earth is in danger of bankruptcy. Make sure your child understands that "bankruptcy" means someone is all out of cash, or resources.

Ask your child if she would like to play a game with you called EARTH BANK. The object of the game is to manage the Earth Bank without going bankrupt.

The Goal

Through a simple game, to demonstrate to your child the limited resources in our "Earth Bank."

Age Range

6 - 10 years

Materials Needed

Monopoly money, a small token, one dice, and game board. (You may wish to photocopy the game board at 140% and set it on the table before you play.)

❖

How to play:

- As the parent, you should be the Banker (at least the first time around). Count out $100 to put in the Earth Bank account, which will be managed by your child.

- Ask your child to put her token on the starting square. She should roll the dice and go forward by that number of squares.

- When she lands on a square, a positive number adds that amount of money to the Earth Bank account. A negative number withdraws that amount of money from the account. Count out the money after each roll of the dice.

- Continue rolling the dice and proceeding until your child's Earth Bank either goes bankrupt or reaches the ending square.

Variations:

1. Switch roles with your child, if she is old enough to count money. You manage the Earth Bank.

2. Assume that your child is managing the Earth Bank for a family of two. In that case, double the amount of each withdrawal. (Deposits remain the same.) How much more quickly does the account go bankrupt?

3. Assume that your child is now managing the Earth Bank for a family of four. Deposits remain the same, but multiply each withdrawal by 4. How far does she get this time before going bankrupt?

Conclusions: Encourage your child to draw conclusions from the game. Has she noticed that at the beginning there are more deposits than withdrawals? Or that towards the end there are more withdrawals? What happens when the earth runs out of resources? What can we do to slow down (or better yet, balance) the process? Can she think of three things she can do to help?

Some ideas include:

- Use bicycles more and cars less
- Use less heat and air conditioning
- Plant more trees
- Plant a garden
- Don't pollute the water
- Don't pollute the air
- Plan to limit the size of her future family to one or two children
- Other

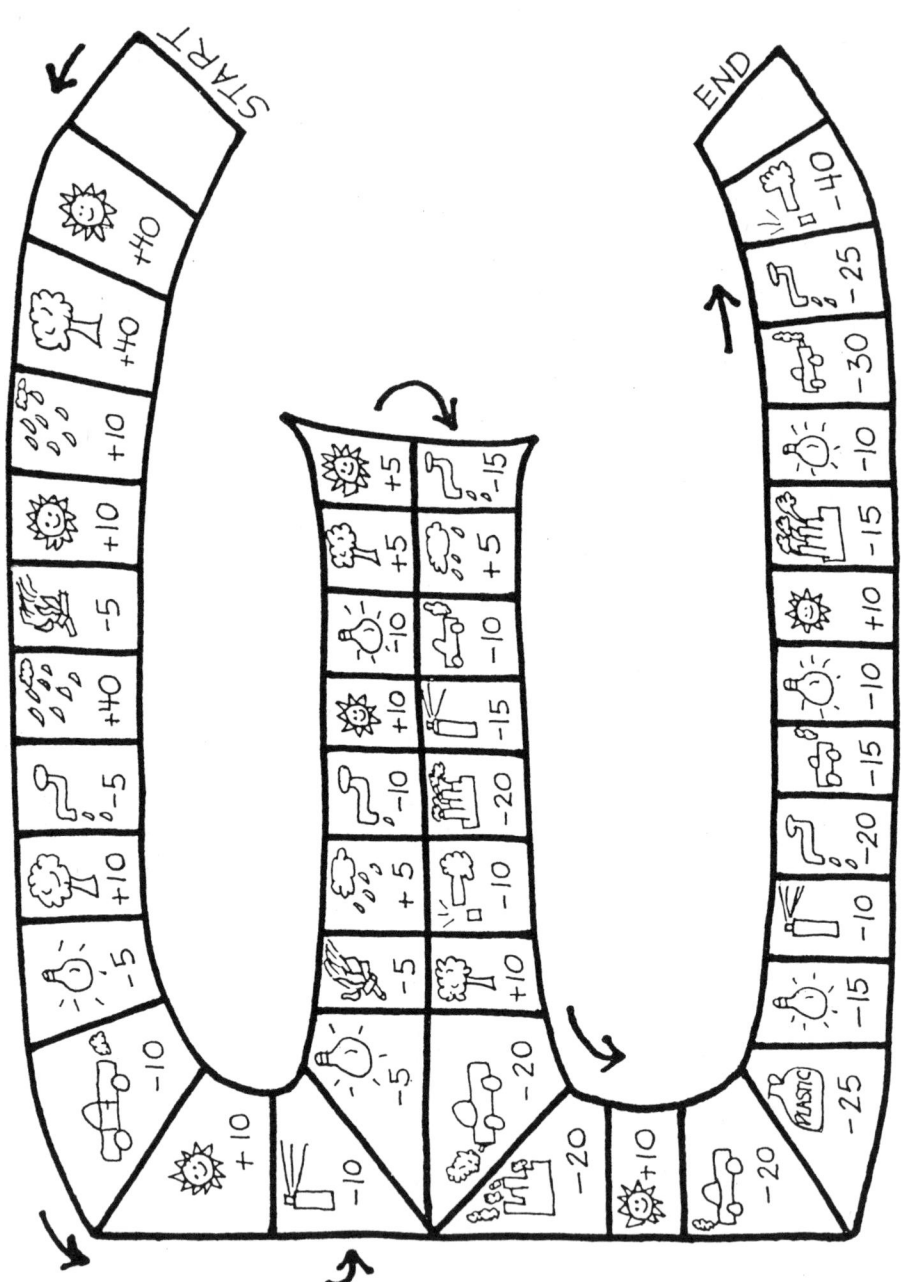

7

THE DANNY TREE

Background

Trees are being cut down in some places as much as four times faster than they are being replaced. We cannot afford to upset the balance between trees and people. Remember, where we use oxygen and produce carbon dioxide, trees use carbon dioxide and produce oxygen. Maintaining enough trees is a matter of survival.

Explain to your child how important trees are. Ask him if he would like to pick one out, name it after himself, and plant it near your house. It will be his responsibility to care for it.

The Goal

To foster your child's appreciation for trees, and to stimulate his interest in caring for them.

Age Range

3 - 5 years

Materials Needed

A small tree, soil, water, shovel, tape measure, paper and pen.

ACTIVITY 1

Take your child to a wooded area and let him pick out a small tree. If this is not feasible, take him to a garden store. Be sure to read any instructions that accompany the tree if you buy it at a store. If you dig one up from a wooded area, see if you can identify it and find information in your encyclopedia that describes where it grows best. Your library is another good source of information.

Find an appropriate place close to your house and ask your child to assist you in planting it. After it's in the ground and you've pressed other soil around its roots, be sure to water it.

ACTIVITY 2

Measure your child with your tape measure. Write his height on a sheet of paper. Now go outside and measure the tree you have named after him (your "Danny" tree). Write down how tall it is in a column beside your child's height.

ACTIVITY 3

Periodically measure both your child and your child's tree. Compare how fast they grow.

Note: If you live in an apartment, you might want to try this with a plant instead of a tree. It won't grow as tall, but it will still stimulate your child's interest in plants. Remember to leave the plant for your child to water each week. It needs to become part of his routine.

8

SUZIE
THE SEAL

Background

The following story presents a problem with no ending—
that's for your child to tell you. Read it to her and let her
decide what happens. She may opt for a happy ending, such
as a person finding Suzie and saving her.

Point out that littering is often fatal to animals, but try not to
unduly alarm your child when conveying the point. She needs
to understand the importance of picking up litter, however.
Any time you can help her retrieve garbage and put it in its
proper place, you will be doing both her and the environment
a huge favor.

Age Range

3 - 7 years

Once upon a time there lived a little seal named Suzie. She
was a very pretty seal, and she liked to play with other seals
during the day. One of her favorite games was to play hide
and seek with her friends.

Sometimes when Suzie swam up to the shore, she saw bright
objects washed up on the beach. Some of them looked sparkly
and mysterious in the sunlight.

"Don't touch those things," said her mother. "It's trash left by
humans, and it can hurt you."

Suzie was disappointed, but she obeyed. She didn't want her
mother to get mad at her.

She stayed away from the cans and plastic bags, but it was

hard. Sometimes the cans floated out into the sea, and they bobbed up and down on the surface of the water. It wasn't easy to avoid them.

Suzie did her best, but one day she came up for air and her head poked through a plastic ring. She didn't see it before it slipped over her neck. It was very tight and she could hardly breathe.

Suzie was upset. She swam around in circles, trying to get it off. Then she swam up to a rock and tried to rub it off. It didn't work, no matter how many times she tried.

Now the plastic ring began to cut into Suzie's skin and make it bleed. She started to cry.

"Mommy, help me," she sobbed.

Her mother circled around Suzie with great sadness. "I can't," she said. "I don't have any arms or fingers. I've seen those plastic rings before. They're what humans use to hold their six-packs of pop together. I don't know why they leave them lying around, where they can kill us. They're impossible to get off."

"What am I going to do?" Suzie whimpered.

Some ideas include:

- A child sees Suzie crying on a rock. She runs to get a pair of scissors from the car and cuts the plastic ring off Suzie's neck. With a grateful smile, Suzie swims back to her mother.

- Suzie's mother rounds up several of her strongest friends, who all have big tusks. The friends slip their tusks under the plastic ring and stretch it until it snaps.

9

HIDDEN WORDS

Background

This kind of activity is ideal for a weekend, when your child has several free hours. Most children love puzzles with hidden words. After your child completes one or both of these puzzles, see if he can define the words on a separate sheet of paper. Be prepared to help. For younger children who complete Puzzle No. 1, you will need to provide assistance in writing definitions.

If your child bogs down at any point, suggest a break. He can always come back to it later. Or promise him a treat when he is through. Praise him when he finishes.

The Goal

To help your child identify and define words that describe issues affecting the earth.

Age Range

5 - 8 years (Puzzle No. 1), 9 - 12 years (Puzzle No. 2)

Materials Needed

Pencil, paper, dictionary, and puzzles on following pages.

Hints: Words in the puzzles are hidden horizontally, vertically, and diagonally. Some are spelled backwards. Also, some of these words are defined in the back of this book in the section called "Questions & Answers."

❖

PUZZLE NO. 1

```
R  F  C  L  E  A  N  A  I  R  U  P
A  E  D  T  S  G  V  R  H  W  W  O
E  B  C  H  E  M  I  C  A  L  S  L
G  O  X  Y  G  E  N  E  I  X  J  L
L  Z  U  T  C  K  S  S  M  O  G  U
A  O  C  L  J  L  R  U  F  Y  A  T
S  N  L  I  C  D  E  N  Q  I  R  I
S  E  L  M  K  R  P  N  C  A  B  O
A  M  B  E  O  A  G  F  H  D  A  N
N  M  T  O  X  I  C  O  Z  O  G  P
Q  G  R  E  E  N  H  O  U  S  E  V
```

Did you find all these words in Puzzle No. 1?

RECYCLE	OXYGEN	CFC	GREENHOUSE
OZONE	GARBAGE	POLLUTION	SMOG
CHEMICALS	RAIN	CLEAN AIR	TOXIC
SUN	GLASS	LIME	SODA

Did you find all these words in Puzzle No. 2?

ENERGY EFFICIENT	GLOBAL	CARBON DIOXIDE
HAZARDOUS WASTE	ENVIRONMENT	BIODEGRADABLE
OZONE DEPLETION	CLOTH	FLUORESCENT
NUCLEAR WASTE	SAVE	BALLOON
OVER POPULATION	ACID RAIN	RECYCLE
LANDFILL	ACTION	ALUMINUM
WARMING	CAR POOL	STYROFOAM
ENERGY CRISIS	GASOLINE	CARE
CONSERVATION	AEROSOLS	GARBAGE
TOXIC CHEMICALS		

PUZZLE NO. 2

```
C F O T S A F E T F X P O A O G L O B A L
B N Z I U L R K M N I A R D I C A P X L U
I P O A P A N W C A E N M N B Q W T V N M
H C N K C S N A G R E C Y C L E O U R O V
A X E L C R O R S L N L S M C L T S K Y P
Z Y D M R L V M L N U C L E A R W A S T E
A D E E P N E I A L O C P D R Y S R T W N
R L P D S E R N C W T B A L L O O N Y Z E
D B L I A B P G I O N I U K E X U Q R J R
O R E X C D O L M R I O A F N P G L O A G
U L T O E I P B E O A D M J O H I B F U Y
S S I I L X U C H N O E L N C V C U O E C
W T O D A U L Y C D B G D I A I X D A T R
A T N N Y F A W C G P R A M R Y J T M F I
S N P O O D T P I X O A R S P H S G L B S
T E M B T Y I E X P L D O L O K R L Q Z I
E M W R S L O S O R E A I H O L I I P A S
R N K A N S N N T D X B P O L F I F J G Q
S O S C P E C L R B R L M N D G E N D A C
T R B S C L C D A R D E V N F S K R E R G
L I G C O P D N O I T C A M E L D Z A B B
N V Y T I M O I W A A L U M I N U M U G H
E N H D O T N E I C I F F E Y G R E N E C
A E Z E M A F N C O N S E R V A T I O N I
```

10

HAZARDOUS WASTE: HAZARDOUS TO YOUR HEALTH!

Background

Most of us don't know what hazardous waste is or how to dispose of it. Dumping it into a landfill or down the kitchen sink could contaminate the ground water. It's important to know which products are hazardous and how to safely dispose of them.

Make sure your child knows that "hazardous" means anything that is potentially dangerous or harmful.

Review these common hazardous items with your child:

1. Paint and paint thinner
2. Oven cleaners
3. Furniture polish
4. Rug and upholstery cleaners
5. Toilet cleaners
6. Pesticides (Raid, Black Flag, etc.)
7. Furniture strippers
8. Car batteries
9. Brake or transmission fluid
10. Antifreeze
11. Mothballs

While we're using these products, they are considered to be hazardous materials. When we throw them out, they become hazardous waste.

Talk to your child about the hazardous materials that are in your home. How many does she think there are? Ask her if she would like to take a trip with you around the house and find the hazardous materials.

The Goal
To help your child identify common hazardous materials in your home and find out how to get rid of them.

Age Range
6 - 9 years

Materials Needed
Black and red pens, self-adhesive labels or paper and scotch tape.

ACTIVITY 1

Draw 25 pictures of a skull and crossed bones, either on the labels or small paper squares. It is the common symbol for poison, and you may want to write "Hazardous" in red letters beneath the symbol if your child is too young.

ACTIVITY 2

Now go through the house with your child and locate any items in the above list. On each item affix the label. Emphasize to your child that these are dangerous products, not **ever** to be played with, swallowed or disposed of in the regular garbage.

ACTIVITY 3

Help your child call the local government authorities and ask them how to dispose of hazardous waste. Be prepared to give them an example of a few items in your house, such as a can of paint. Perhaps there is a recycling agency, a licensed contractor, or a wastewater treatment plant nearby that will handle the waste. Ask for a name and telephone number of the agency, and then call them to confirm the information.

ACTIVITY 4

When you have information about how to dispose of several types of hazardous waste, have your child write it down in the front of your telephone book. Then, when you are ready to dispose of the waste, follow the instructions you have noted. You'll feel good about protecting the environment from such dangerous chemicals.

11

RAP

Background

Your child is probably familiar with the rhythmic sounds of Rap. The following verses can be said in Rap form, accompanied by clapping or snapping of the fingers. Be creative, vary the rhythm, and have fun. If your child is musically inclined and you own a musical instrument, let him experiment with it.

The Goal

To personalize your child's desire to stop hurting the earth through repetition and rhythm.

Age Range

6 - 10 years

Materials Needed

Rap sheet, your fingers, and a musical instrument (optional).

Variations: Write your own verses to add to this Rap, or create a new Rap.

Invite your child's friends to do this Rap with him. Teach them the words and help them the first few times—then see if they can do it on their own.

RAP

Gonna stop, gonna stop, gonna stop right now
If it's hurtin' the earth we're gonna stop it right now
Right now, uh-huh

Don't care about the time, don't care about the cost
If it's hurtin' the earth we're gonna stop it right now
Right now, uh-huh

You'd better watch out, we're onto your game
Gonna keep after you till you stop, stop, stop
Hurtin' the earth
Gonna stop you right now, right now, uh-huh

Gonna stop, gonna stop, gonna stop right now
If it's hurtin' the earth we're gonna stop it right now
Right now, uh-huh, right now, UH-HUH!!!

12

EARTH POEMS

Background

Most children enjoy poems, especially the familiar ones they've grown up with. It's fun when poems rhyme, but they don't have to. They can be any combination of words that expresses a thought, no matter how simple.

Ask your child if she would like to listen to some earth poems and then try some of her own. Remember, her poems don't have to be anything more than thoughts about ways to help the earth.

The Goal

To increase your child's awareness of the environment and her desire to protect it through poetry.

Age Range

7 - 10 years

Materials Needed

Paper and pencil, crayons (optional).

ACTIVITY 1

Read the following poems to your child. Ask her to close her eyes as you read and imagine what's happening. Talk about each one.

ACTIVITY 2

Ask your child if she can write a poem about protecting the

earth. It could be about making the environment safe for animals, such as her favorite pet. It could be about keeping the flowers and the street clean. Let her be as creative as she wishes.

ACTIVITY 3

After she finishes her poem, ask her if she would like to illustrate it. She could do a simple line sketch when her pencil, or use crayons. When she is through, praise her and post the poem on your refrigerator or wherever else it will attract attention.

I'M A LITTLE FISH

I'm a little fish
swimming in the sea.
All I want when I grow up
is a chance to be free.

I want my world
to be fresh and clear,
Not littered with trash
and plagued by fear.

Give me a chance
to play all day,
And live my life
In the happiest way.

I'm a little fish
swimming in the sea,
I need you to help—
Please, won't you help me?

A MAGIC BOND

Today I sat beneath the tree
that my mother planted for me
It was a long time ago,
so long I can hardly remember it

I sat on the lawn
and my back touched the bark
The sun poked between leaves
and made patterns on my face

I closed my eyes
and smelled the newly cut grass
Somewhere in the distance I heard
a lawn mower churning

And while I listened
I thought I could hear
my tree talking to me

Was it the wind?
Or was it a sigh?
It sounded happy, whatever it was

I breathed out
My tree breathed in
And we exchanged whispers

My tree and I
We have a Magic Bond
We can't live without each other

THE RAIN

Some people don't like the rain
      --   it's inconvenient
      --   it messes up their hair
      --   it gets their clothes wet

But me, I like the rain
      --   it splashes my face
      --   it cleans the earth
      --   it makes puddles to walk through

From my bedroom window, I look outside
      --   I feel the cool puffs of air on my skin
      --   I watch the drops dance on the street
      --   I laugh as people scurry inside

Me? I like the rain
      --   it sounds like a drum on my roof
      --   it makes me feel cozy inside
      --   it puts me to sleep

And it gives the earth a drink.

13

COLLAGES: EARTH FRIENDLY/ EARTH UNFRIENDLY

Background

Sometimes it's hard to tell the difference between things that hurt the environment and things that help the environment. Pictures can make the difference more clear.

Ask your child if he can identify some things that are earth friendly. Some examples might be:

Earth Friendly Things

Bicycles	Lakes
Animals	Mountains
Vegetables	Parks
Rain	The sun
Trees	Plants
Rivers	Fruits

Can he think of more?

Earth Unfriendly Things

Smoke	Cars
Dirty water	Dirty air
Too many people	Chemicals
Trash	Throw-away items
Styrofoam	Aerosol sprays
Pesticides	Air conditioners
Gasoline	Dead trees

Can he think of more?

Ask your child if he would like to make collages that include earth friendly and unfriendly items. If he's never seen a collage, explain that it's a collection of pictures arranged on a sheet of paper. The pictures may be arranged at different angles, and some usually overlap others.

The Goal

To create two collages from magazine and newspaper pictures, the first with items that are earth friendly, and the second with items that are earth unfriendly.

Age Range

5 - 9 years

Materials Needed

Two poster boards (one green, the other gray), old magazines, old newspapers, scissors, paste.

ACTIVITY 1

Ask your child to cut out pictures of things that are earth friendly and paste them on the green poster board. Help him label it "EARTH FRIENDLY." Arrange them in an attractive pattern. Be prepared to answer questions as your child progresses, especially if he has a difficult time telling the difference between earth friendly and unfriendly things.

ACTIVITY 2

Next, ask your child to cut out pictures of things that are earth unfriendly. Paste them on the gray poster board, and label it "EARTH UNFRIENDLY."

ACTIVITY 3

Display the two collages in your child's bedroom or some other place in the house.

14

GARDEN FRESH SOUP

Background

Americans eat a lot of meat and never stop to think how much it impacts the earth. For example, did you know that it takes 16 pounds of grains and 2500 gallons of water to make one pound of beef? Nearly one-third of North America is used for raising cattle, and more than half of our water is used to produce livestock. Grazing animals also produce methane, which contributes to the greenhouse effect. Eating vegetables, grains and fruits is a more earth friendly way to live.

How much meat you eat is up to you. But any time you can substitute vegetarian meals for meat dishes you will help save the earth's resources.

Talk to your child about how much water and grain are used to produce meat. Explain that by eating some meals without meat, we can conserve water and food and energy. Also, these vegetarian meals are good for you because they usually don't contain as much fat as meat dishes.

Ask your child if she would like to create her own Garden Fresh Soup. It should contain lots of vegetables, potatoes and pasta—but no meat. The recipe would be a special one that she invents all by herself.

The Goal

To serve at least two or three vegetarian dinners every month.

Age Range

6 - 12

Materials Needed

Celery, carrots, broccoli, potatoes, cabbage, peppers, tomatoes, pasta, water, large pot, spices, tomato juice, butter, cheese, other vegetables as desired.

ACTIVITY 1

Talk to your child about what ingredients she would like to include in her Garden Fresh Soup. Let her select them at the grocery store, and plan to allow two or three hours to make the soup. A Saturday afternoon might be ideal. Supervise your child and assist whenever necessary, but allow her as much freedom as you can. Here are some guidelines:

1. Pour three to four cups of water into the pot and put it on the stove, on medium heat.

2. Add the tomato juice to the water and stir. Bring to a boil.

3. Wash vegetables and potatoes. Cut them into cube sized squares. Add them to the water in your pot.

4. Add spices to taste. Some favorites are: Salt, pepper, poultry seasoning, Mrs. Dash, hot sauce, parsley.

5. Taste the soup to see if you should add any more spices, vegetables, or water.

6. Reduce the heat to low and let it simmer for an hour.

7. Then add a handful of pasta to the soup and stir.

8. Let the soup simmer for another 30 minutes and then turn off the heat.

9. Add a teaspoon of butter to the soup.

10. Serve soup for dinner, garnished with grated cheese and parsley. Also serve salad, rolls, and a light dessert.

11. If you wish, make notes about how your soup tasted, and whether you would do anything differently next time. Don't be afraid to keep experimenting until you get it just the way you like it. There's nothing wrong with a little creativity and variety. Have fun with it.

ACTIVITY 2

Clean up the kitchen together (you guessed it!)

ACTIVITY 3

In subsequent weeks or months, make other soups using your favorite ingredients.

15

SINKING CITIES

Background

Although the air we breathe is made up mostly of oxygen and nitrogen, there are traces of other gases in it. These traces are very small, but they are important. Like a greenhouse, they trap heat from the earth and keep it from escaping into space. However, the more gases there are in the air, the more heat is retained.

The danger is that too many gases will enter the air, and the earth's temperature will get too hot. Scientists call this the greenhouse effect.

The main culprits are:

- *Carbon Dioxide*, from burning fossil fuels like oil, coal and natural gas

- *Methane* from cattle and landfills

- *Nitrous Oxide* from burning wood and fossil fuels and the microbes that break down chemical fertilizers

These gases will cause higher temperatures that could turn farms into deserts, melt ice caps, raise the sea level, and sink coastal cities. It is a long range process that could take 50-100 years to produce dramatic changes.

Talk to your child about the greenhouse effect and how it threatens our climate. Discuss the culprits that cause it, and ask him to start thinking about ways to control it.

The Goal

To demonstrate one aspect of the greenhouse effect to your child, and to teach him three things he can do to help stop it.

Age Range
    5 - 8 years

Materials Needed
    A square of wood, about 12" x 12", aluminum foil, Play Dough, paper and pen, scotch tape.

ACTIVITY 1

Ask your child to cover the square of wood in tin foil. Then let him build a city of Play Dough on top of the tin foil. He should shape houses along the edges, and perhaps include a hill in the center.

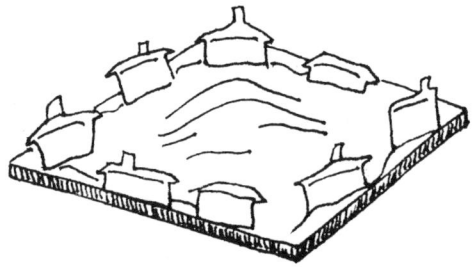

Variation: Instead of a city, ask an older child to form the outline of the United States. The coastal areas should be lower than the center. Raise a few areas to represent homes.

ACTIVITY 2

Help your child place the square in the kitchen sink. Plug the drain. Let him run enough water so that it collects around the edge but does not cover much of his Play Dough city.

Now, ask him to pretend that the temperature is increasing and the ice caps are starting to melt. Let him run more water, until it begins to creep up on the city and sink some of the homes.

Run more water, until all of the edges are under water. Ask your child what will happen to the homes and people on the edge or coast. Where will they go? What will they do?

Do you live near an ocean? Or do you know someone who does? Discuss it with your child.

Let him cover as much of the city as he likes with water. Then take it out of the sink, press the Play Dough into a ball and put it away.

ACTIVITY 3

Ask your child to name three things he can do to help stop the greenhouse effect. Help him write them on a list and tape it beside his bed (or wherever he will see it often).

Some ideas include:

• Combine trips to the store so the car is used less often

• Plant a tree

• Grow some indoor plants

• Ride a bicycle whenever possible instead of using the car

• Reduce the number of fires in your fireplace during the winter

• Eat two or three vegetarian meals every month

• Other

16

DIAPERING DOLLS

Background

Disposable diapers use a huge amount of wood pulp and plastic. They occupy about 1% of the space in landfills, including millions of tons of feces and urine. These disposable diapers can take up to 500 years to decompose. In the meantime, they contain dangerous viruses that could contaminate our ground water.

Cloth diapers, in comparison, can decompose in 1 to 6 months. The feces and urine in them are properly disposed of in septic tanks or sewage treatment plants. And after cloth diapers wear out, they are easily recycled into rags.

Although cloth diapers use water and energy when washed, they are still more earth friendly than disposable diapers. Disposable diapers use more wood to produce, occupy more space in landfills, and have the potential to pollute the environment.

Explain to your child why cloth diapers are more earth friendly than disposable diapers. Tailor your explanation to her ability to understand.

Make sure she knows that a diaper service collects dirty diapers from a family each week, washes them, dries and folds them, and returns them to the family to re-use. Explain that many parents use a diaper service because they do not have time to wash the diapers themselves. Now ask your child if she would like to play a diaper service game with you and one of her dolls.

The Goal

To teach your child why cloth diapers are more earth friendly than disposable diapers, and to encourage her to use cloth diapers on her dolls.

Age Range
3 - 6 years

Materials Needed
Scraps of cloth from old pillowcases or other garments, pins, your child's doll(s), can with a make-shift lid.

ACTIVITY 1

Help your child bathe her doll (if it's water resistant). Assist her in putting the cloth diaper and safety pin around her doll's waist. The dirty diapers should be stored in a covered can.

ACTIVITY 2

Pretend you are the diaper service. Knock on the door and let your child open it. Greet her and tell her you are there to collect this week's dirty diapers. She should give you the can. Accept it and pretend to leave.

ACTIVITY 3

Ask your child to help you be part of the diaper service. She should assist you in bringing the can to your laundry area. If you are ready to wash a load of your own clothes, add the diapers to your wash. (Remember, they're not really dirty).

ACTIVITY 4

When the diapers are washed, drape them over a hanger or hang them up to dry. Explain that this saves electricity. After they're dry, fold them and deliver them to your child—with a smile.

17

THE FRIENDLY GREEN GHOST

Read the following story to your child at bedtime or any other time that's convenient. (Ideal age range is 6 - 10). At the end, ask him what he thinks the Friendly Green Ghost would say about your family.

Scott Trumble lived with his mother and father in a house that was almost 100 years old. But Scott didn't mind because the house had an attic and all kinds of secret places. Sometimes when his friends spent the night, they slept in the attic under Army blankets. It was fun to read by flashlight and tell ghost stories and crunch on peanut M&Ms.

"I bet you'd be too scared to sleep up here by yourself," said Robert, one of Scott's friends.

"No wayyyy," Scott bragged.

"Then I dare you," Robert said.

Scott laughed. It was a shaky laugh. "If my parents say it's OK, I will," he said.

But Scott's mom was in a bad mood the next morning. She had spent ten minutes combing her hair into place, and when she went to spray her curls with hair spray, her aerosol can wouldn't work. The nozzle was jammed, even though it was a brand new can. She shook it and shook it, but still it wouldn't spray. And several other cans were mysteriously out of order, too.

"Have you been messing with my hair spray, young man?" she snapped.

"No," Scott said. "I haven't touched it."

"Well, it worked fine yesterday," his mother said, banging her can against the sink.

"Where are my styrofoam cups?" Scott's dad hollered from the doorway. "I put them right at the top of the stairs so I wouldn't forget them on my way to work."

Both parents looked at Scott.

"I didn't touch them," Scott said. "Honest!"

"Then we must have a ghost in the house," his dad said sarcastically.

It didn't seem like a good time to ask for special privileges. Scott decided to wait.

That night after dinner he cleared the table and tossed the garbage in the trash can as usual. He carried the dishes to the kitchen and rinsed them off. When he returned to the dining room, he noticed that the pop cans were sitting on top of the table in a neat row.

"I thought I just threw them out," Scott frowned. He grabbed them and stuffed them into the trash can. He watched for a minute to make sure they stayed there, and then he left the room.

A couple minutes later he poked his head in the dining room, and the pop cans were on top of the table. It was weird. His parents were outside on the porch and he knew they hadn't come into the house. Scott felt goose bumps stand up on his arms.

Other strange things happened, too. When he left a room the light flickered off, even though he didn't touch the switch. And when he took a shower, the water pressure slowed to a dribble—even when the faucet was turned on all the way.

With all the odd things happening around the house, Scott probably would have forgotten about spending the night in the attic. But Robert teased him in front of his friends at school, and that reminded him. That evening he asked his parents for permission to sleep upstairs on Friday night.

"Seems like kind of a crazy thing to do," his dad said. "But it's OK by me, I guess."

Scott waited to go to the attic until he was so tired his eyes wouldn't stay open. Then he changed into his pajamas, grabbed his pillow and climbed the stairs.

The door creaked as it opened, and a gust of cool air brushed his face. He spread out his blankets on the floor and wrapped himself up like a cocoon. After the light was off he tried not to think about anything scary.

Sometime in the middle of the night he awoke. At his feet was a glowing green ghost. It sounded like it was sighing. Scott thought he must be dreaming so he rubbed his eyes. But when he opened them again, the ghost was still there. This time it looked directly at him and frowned.

"Are you going to slime me?" Scott asked.

"Slime you?" the green ghost said. "What's that?"

"You know—splash me and get me all gooey with that green stuff you're wearing. I saw it happen in 'Ghostbusters.'"

"Of course not," the ghost said. It sighed again and crossed its legs. "Although that might not be such a bad idea. At least it would get your attention. As it is, I spend all my time trying to train you and your parents not to be so wasteful. It's wearing me out."

"What do you mean?" Scott asked. "We don't waste things."

"HA!" the ghost sputtered. It pointed a long green finger at him. "You waste electricity and water, you don't recycle your trash, and you use products that hurt the earth. It took me *years* to get the last family that lived here straightened out. And as soon as I did, they moved. Now I'm stuck with you Trumbles. I don't know if I have the energy to whip you into shape."

"So *you're* the one who's been doing all these weird things," Scott said. "My parents thought it was me."

"Actually, that's not such a bad idea," the ghost said. "I could use an assistant." It stood up and began to float around the room. Its body cast green shadows on the wall. "You could start being more friendly to the earth yourself, and then you could help me re-train your parents. I'll give you some pointers."

"I don't know," Scott said. "I'm just a kid. My parents will never listen to me."

The ghost winked. "Yes, they will," it whispered. "I'll guarantee it." With a graceful motion, it returned to the end of Scott's blanket and began to tell him how to protect the earth.

"By the way, what should I call you?" Scott asked, when it was through.

"Oh, I don't really have a name," the ghost replied. "Just call me the Friendly Green Ghost, if you have to call me something."

The next morning Scott waited until his mother started to spray her hair with a new can of hair spray.

"You know, Mom, that stuff is wrecking the ozone layer," he said. "You shouldn't use it. Maybe you could use the non-aerosol kind that has a pump, instead of this one."

Scott's mother turned toward him and raised her eyebrow. She was about to snap at him when her mouth suddenly curved up at the corners. "You're right," she smiled. "I'll go buy the non-aerosol kind today and get rid of this one."

Scott was amazed. He looked up at the light and thought he saw a green glow around the bulb.

After breakfast he helped his father rinse the dishes. He noticed that his father left the water running while he wiped the kitchen table and put away the milk.

"You waste a lot of water that way, Dad," Scott pointed out.

"Some day the earth is going to run out. Maybe you could turn off the faucet unless you're using it."

Scott's dad looked like he was going to bark at him. Instead, he nodded. "Guess you're right, son. I won't do that anymore."

"Wow," Scott smiled. This was working better than he imagined. The Friendly Green Ghost must be looking out for him.

"You know, Dad, I think you and Mom should take me to Disneyland this summer," he said.

"No, I don't think so," his father said. "We don't have enough money."

"Darn!" Scott said. Apparently the ghost's powers didn't cover other kinds of requests.

Over the next several months Scott and the Friendly Green Ghost talked many times. And little by little the Trumbles changed their habits until they became an earth friendly family.

The Friendly Green Ghost was very happy. It no longer had to work so hard, so there was more time to relax. It snacked on peanut M&Ms that Scott left in the attic, and at last count it had gained ten pounds.

"This is the way it should be," it burped.

THE END

18

GREEN GHOST ART

Background
Review the Friendly Green Ghost story with your child and ask her if she would like to illustrate it. She could choose to draw a picture of one event or several. Mention some possibilities:

- Scott's mom spraying her hair with a can of aerosol hair spray

- The Friendly Green Ghost sitting on Scott's blanket while he is in the attic

- The Friendly Green Ghost doing any of these things:
  - turning off a water faucet
  - separating aluminum cans from other trash
  - hiding styrofoam cups
  - turning off lights

- The Friendly Green Ghost showing Scott's parents how to be more earth friendly

- The Friendly Green Ghost eating peanut M&Ms.

The Goal
To reinforce some of the concepts in the Friendly Green Ghost story.

Age Range
6 - 10 years

Materials Needed
Paper, crayons, pencil or markers.

❖

ACTIVITY 1

After you and your child talk about several possibilities, let her draw the desired number of pictures. She may want you to admire them, so be prepared to praise her efforts.

ACTIVITY 2

Perhaps your child is artistic enough to draw a series of cartoons. In that case she may want to add the balloons that include simple sentences of dialogue.

ACTIVITY 3

When the pictures are finished, ask her to explain them to you. She may add other details or embroider the story to include other "Boo-Boos" that the Trumbles committed before they became an earth friendly family. Encourage her creativity. When she is finished, tape them to a wall somewhere in your house.

19

YOUNG ACTIVISTS

Background

The environment is threatened daily by people's carelessness and ignorance. By calling attention to the conditions around us, we affect the way other people treat the earth. All we need is a willingness to speak out.

There are plenty of environmental concerns in every community. Interest your child in them. Encourage him to watch news stories about them, read articles in the newspaper, or attend meetings. For example:

- Is your city planning to plant trees in an area of town that doesn't have any?

- Is your city running out of room at its landfill?

- Is your city's air pollution in violation of federal standards?

- Are there rivers or streams in your community that are dirty?

- Does your city have a recycling program?

- Does your community need a diaper service?

- Does your city need to improve its bicycle paths?

Personalize these issues by discussing their effects on your child. For instance, polluted air means your child may develop lung cancer at an early age. Is that acceptable?

Explain to him that some good ways to stop environmental abuses are to write letters to the local newspaper, call public officials, or testify at public meetings.

The Goal
To encourage your child to identify a local issue that affects the earth, and to speak out about it.

Age Range
8 - 12 years

Materials Needed
Paper and pen, or telephone.

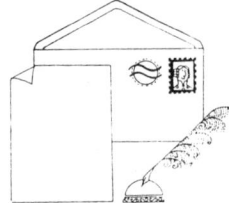

❖

ACTIVITY 1

After you have identified a concern that interests your child, ask him if he would like to write a letter to the editor of your local newspaper. He should express his views in a clear manner, and he should also include his age somewhere in the letter. Here's an example:

Dear Editor:

My name is Brad. I am 9 years old. I don't like to see trees being cut down. I also don't like air pollution. I don't like the styrofoam that fast food joints give you their food in. Pretty soon there won't be anything left on earth but trash.

I heard our landfill is already full. Where are we going to dump our trash after that? Adults want us to be responsible, but a lot of them are not teaching us by example.

Sincerely,
Brad Casey
22 Aurora Drive
Fairfield, Missouri

ACTIVITY 2

Perhaps a phone call to an elected official would get results. If so, work with your child to identify key points he wants to make during the call. Supervise the call and be prepared to intervene if necessary.

ACTIVITY 3

Is testimony being taken by your city council about an environmental issue? If your child wants to speak to the council about it, take him to the council chambers. Often there's a sign-up sheet at the door. Let him write down his name and address. When it's his turn, accompany him to the microphone if he wishes. Make sure he brings a paper with him that outlines his key points. If he's confident enough he might prefer to speak off the cuff. You'll be surprised how effective a simple, heartfelt message is. Be sure to praise your child after he has testified and you're alone again.

ACTIVITY 4

Continue to monitor environmental issues in your community. Whenever there is an opportunity to speak out, encourage your child to do so. His confidence will grow each time.

A word of caution: Be prepared for some degree of self-examination as your child's conscience develops. He may call some of your own inconsistencies into question. If he does and you act on it, you will both grow from the experience.

20

YOUNG VOLUNTEERS

Background

America has so many environmental problems that the government will never be able to solve them all. Very often it is a private citizen who takes the first step to solve a problem. This person reaches out to other people and forms a group to take action. These volunteers are some of our best weapons in the fight against pollution.

Many communities have a Volunteer Center that recruits and places volunteers in non-profit organizations. These Volunteer Centers specialize in matching the talents of individuals with the needs of organizations. Your local United Way would be a good place to start. Ask if they have a Volunteer Action Center. If they don't, ask where you might find such a service.

Perhaps you already know of an environmental organization in your community. If you do, call and ask if they need volunteers. Be sure to include questions about the time commitment, nature of the volunteer activity, what kind of supervision is provided, and whether it's something the whole family could do together. It's always a good idea to visit the organization ahead of time to meet the people and get a clear idea of what the organization does.

Ask your child if she knows what a volunteer is. If she doesn't, explain that it's a person who does a task without

being paid. She might wonder why someone would work for free. Point out that there are many benefits to volunteering besides getting paid. These benefits include:

- A sense of satisfaction from doing something important
- The pleasure of working with other people who care about the same things you do
- Making new friends
- Getting involved in your community
- Developing new skills, abilities, and contacts
- Becoming a more confident, interesting person

Ask your child if she would like to volunteer for a project with you. She could help pick the organization and project, so it would be a task she is interested in.

The Goal
To involve your child as a volunteer in an organization whose activities protect the environment.

Age Range
5 - 12+

Materials Needed
None

ACTIVITY 1

After you have identified the organization for which you would like to volunteer, set up a schedule. Take your child to the organization at the appointed time. If at all possible, perform the volunteer task(s) with her.

- Some types of volunteer tasks might include:
- Picking up litter along the highway
- Planting flowers

- Hauling aluminum cans to a recycling center
- Putting up environmental posters around town
- Mailing information to people
- Separating different colors of glass at a recycling collection site

Be sure that the activity is one that challenges your child, is appropriate to her age level, and does not unduly tire her. Remember to reinforce her sense of satisfaction for performing an important duty.

ACTIVITY 2

If your city does not have an environmental group that needs volunteers, don't be discouraged. There are a lot of informal volunteer activities that your child can do. For example, she could spend an hour a week picking up trash from the sides of the road in your neighborhood. Plan to accompany her on these trips, and when you find items that are recyclable (such as aluminum cans), separate them in different containers. Later you can take them with your other aluminum cans to the recycling center.

21

ENVIRONMENTAL AUDIT

Background

Identifying the sources of pollution in our own homes is sometimes a difficult thing to do. It's easy to condemn pollution in the global sense—but it's another thing to face up to the environmental damage we cause every day.

Make sure your child knows the definition of an "audit." In business terms it means "to check the correctness of accounts." Used here, its purpose is to check the correctness of your home in environmental terms.

Discuss some household items that are either friendly or unfriendly to the earth. Explain to your child that the goal of this Environmental Audit is to find out how earth friendly or unfriendly your home is. Some examples are:

Earth Friendly Things in Your Home

- Plants
- Flowers
- A system to separate garbage for recycling
- Bicycles
- Bird feeders
- A washer with side loading
- Trees in the yard
- Low flow shower head on the showers
- Energy efficient insulation
- Cloth diapers, if there is a baby in the family

- Other

Can he think of more?

Earth Unfriendly Things in Your Home

- Disposable razor blades
- Throw-away flashlights or cameras
- Aerosol hair spray
- Pesticides (Raid, Black Flag, etc.)
- Disposable diapers
- Paper or plastic plates
- Styrofoam cups
- Plastic utensils
- More than 1 refrigerator
- Paint and paint thinner
- Oven cleaners
- Furniture polish
- Toilet cleaners
- Wood burning stove without controls
- Other

Can he think of more?

Be prepared to discuss why these items are friendly or un-friendly. For example, when used properly furniture polish may be considered friendly, but it becomes hazardous waste when we have to dispose of it. And any product that is meant to be thrown away after one use is wasteful. It increases the trash in our landfills.

Now that your child is familiar with earth friendly and unfriendly items in the home, ask her if she would like to find out how friendly your home is. She would need to go on a home tour with you and help point out items that are either friendly or unfriendly.

The Goal

To help your child identify the friendly and unfriendly effects we have on the environment in our home; and to arrive at a score that tells you how earth friendly your home is.

Age Range

6 - 10 years

Materials Needed

Paper and pencil.

ACTIVITY 1

Ask your child to divide his paper into two columns. On the right side of the column, draw a happy face. On the left side of the column, draw an unhappy face.

Tour your home with your child. For each earth friendly item you find, put a mark in the happy column. For each earth unfriendly item you find, put a mark in the unhappy column.

Be as thorough as time allows. You may choose to put one mark for each flower in your flower box, or only one. It's up to you how detailed to get.

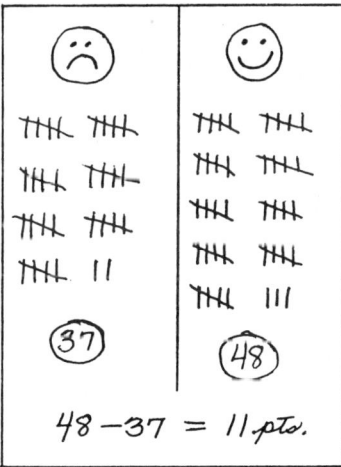

ACTIVITY 2

Add up the marks in your happy column. Then add up the marks in your unhappy column. Subtract the unhappy marks from the total number of happy marks. What was your score? Did you find that there were more unfriendly items than friendly items? Or the other way around?

Talk to your child about the results of your Environmental Audit. Are there things you can do to reduce the number of unfriendly items in your home? If you have trouble reducing the number of unfriendly items, perhaps you could change the balance by adding earth friendly items. Or perhaps you could find friendly substitutes for unfriendly items. See what suggestions your child has, and be prepared to try a couple of the feasible ones.

SCORES

- 100 or more	Your home is extremely unfriendly
- 75 to -99	Your home is very unfriendly
- 50 to -74	Your home is moderately unfriendly
- 25 to -49	Your home is mildly unfriendly
- 1 to -24	Your home is almost friendly; with a little more effort you'll get there
+ 0 to 24	Your home is friendly
+ 25 to 49	Your home is very friendly
+ 50 to 74	Your home is extremely friendly
+ 75 to 99	Your home is extraordinarily friendly
+100 or more	CONGRATULATIONS!!! Your home is a model home. Treat yourself and your child to something special and KEEP UP THE GOOD WORK.

22

ECOLOGY COP

Background

Does your child know what "Ecology" means? If not, ask her to look it up in a dictionary. She may want to write down the definition so that it becomes part of her vocabulary. In her words, ecology might mean:

- "The way living things and the earth get along together."

An older child might understand this definition:

- "The branch of biology that deals with the relation of living things to their environment and to each other."

Ask your child what an Ecology Cop might be concerned with. If she says something like, "offenses that people commit toward the environment," she's right on target.

Agree in advance on specific offenses that will receive a ticket from the Ecology Cop. Some examples are:

Offenses

- Failure to turn off a light when you leave a room for more than 5 minutes
- Opening the refrigerator door for more than 30 seconds at a time
- Taking a shower that lasts more than 7 minutes (or where the water runs consecutively for more than 7 minutes)
- Using a paper towel instead of a cloth towel
- Using an aerosol hair spray or deodorant
- Leaving the water running when you brush your teeth or wash your face
- Failure to recycle aluminum cans, glass or newspaper
- Using disposable diapers on the baby

- Using the car unnecessarily, when either a bicycle would suffice or public transportation is available

- Improperly disposing of hazardous wastes

- Setting your home's air conditioning too low (72 or lower)

- Forgetting to take paper bags to the store with you when you shop

- Accepting food in styrofoam containers at a fast food restaurant

- Washing clothes without a full load

TICKET

Issued to _____

Date _____

Offense _____

_____

signed _____

Ecology Cop

The Goal
To help your child recognize offenses that hurt the earth and to write tickets for each offense.

Age Range
7 - 12 years

Materials Needed
Pen, several tickets (similar to the illustration), two jars, 25 coins (either pennies, nickels, dimes or quarters) and a badge.

Before you start: Label one jar with your child's name and the other with the word "Donation." Fill your child's jar with 25 coins.

ACTIVITY 1

If there is one child in your family, let her be the Ecology Cop for the weekend. She should wear a badge while she is "on duty." Her task is to catch you or your spouse in a finable offense. When she does, she should fill out a ticket and hand it to you. Be sure to act chagrined and tell her she's just too sharp for you. (Don't be annoyed, or the game will cease to be fun.) For each ticket you receive, put a coin in the jar marked "Donation."

ACTIVITY 2

Now you be the Ecology Cop for a day or weekend. Ticket your child whenever she commits a finable offense. Every time she is ticketed, she needs to remove one coin from the jar with her name on it and drop it into the jar marked "Donation."

ACTIVITY 3

If you have more than one child, rotate the function of Ecology Cop between them. (Also use a separate jar of coins for each child.) Explain that the Cop on duty must be treated with respect, and that any squabbles will result in a double fine to both of them—regardless of who is at fault.

ACTIVITY 4

Trade places with your child, or rotate the Ecology Cop between children, as often as you like. When you decide to give the game a rest, let your child keep the coins in the jar with her name. The jar marked "Donation" should be donated to the environmental charity of your child's choice. Get paper rolls from a bank and roll the coins before you hand carry the donation to your charity. Or deposit them in your bank account and write a check.

23

KING FOR A DAY

Background

Choose a time when you and your child can spend at least 30 minutes together. Bedtime might be ideal. Ask him to imagine that he is King of the World. His job includes being fair to everyone and protecting the environment so that it stays healthy for all the people. Most of the time it is peaceful in his kingdom, but every now and then a problem arises that he needs to solve. Pose the following problems to your child and ask what he, as King, would do.

Explain that the air, water, wildlife and environment are sometimes referred to as the "commons." That is, they are resources owned commonly by the people. Usually the government manages them. In this case, that's the King's job.

Suggestions: Don't make the problems easy for your child. He may propose a simple solution. If he does, challenge him. Ask him to think about the consequences of his solution. What will happen if he chooses a certain course of action? Or another? Compare the effects. It's possible that short-term solutions may not be good in the long run. Remember, the King needs to be fair at the same time he protects the environment.

The Goal

To develop your child's problem-solving abilities in relation to the environment.

Age Range
6 - 9 years

Materials Needed
None

Problem 1

A factory in the eastern part of the kingdom makes a lot of food. But it also adds chemicals to some of the food. To get rid of the chemicals after it uses them, the factory discharges them in the river behind its building. The river has started to turn orange and fish are dying.

One of the king's assistants has already told the factory to quit dumping these chemicals in the river. But the factory president says it has no where else to get rid of the chemicals. He says it costs so much to dispose of the chemicals anywhere else that if the king forces him to stop, he will have to shut down his factory. And if he shuts down his factory, there won't be enough food for the kingdom and several hundred people will lose their jobs. He thinks the king should tell his assistant to let him alone so the chemicals can keep being dumped in the river. What should the king do?

Possible Solution: **The King could ask the factory president to meet with his top environmental advisers. They could teach the factory president about a new method for treating chemicals before they are discharged into the water. The King might offer to pay part of the expense for this method so that the factory wouldn't go broke. That way no one would lose his job and the water would be clean when it was discharged into the river.**

Problem 2

The ozone layer above the kingdom is disappearing. That means that portions of the sun's energy known as ultraviolet rays are passing through the atmosphere. The King knows this is dangerous because ultraviolet rays can cause skin cancer. It's the summertime and people are very hot. To cool down, they are using air conditioners in their homes and cars. They have also bought more refrigerators to store cool drinks. The king knows that these items can cause the ozone layer to disappear even faster. He has asked his people to try to live with less air conditioning and refrigerators, but they say they can't. It's too uncomfortable. What should the king do?

Possible Solutions: The King could run ads on TV that show the dangers of letting the ozone layer disappear. The ads would educate people so that they would stop using too much air conditioning.

The King could also bring people together with his environmental advisers. Together they could pass laws that limited the use of things that produce CFCs, because CFCs harm the ozone layer.

Another thing the King could do is give more money to research groups that are trying to find safe alternatives to the CFCs used in air conditioners.

Problem 3

The kingdom's landfills are all full. There is no where else to put trash, so one company has started taking it out to sea and dumping it into the ocean. The seals and whales and dolphins and turtles are swallowing it and dying. Also, the fish are so diseased that when they are caught and sold to people, the people who eat them also get sick. No one really wants to keep dumping trash in the ocean, but they aren't sure what else to do. What should the king do?

Possible Solutions: The King could start a recycling program. Perhaps some incentives could be used, such as paying people money for recycling their trash. And fines could be imposed on people who didn't recycle.

Another part of this program could be educating the people about conservation, so that there would be less trash in the first place. People could learn to use earth friendly products, such as biodegradable cloth diapers. This would cut down on the amount of trash that needed to be disposed of.One alternative would be to burn trash in an incinerator. However, this would have to be closely monitored because it could cause air pollution.

In addition, the King could order all ocean dumping to stop at once. Anyone caught dumping trash into the ocean would be fined or thrown in jail.

Until the ocean was cleaned up, fish would have to be tested and not eaten if they were contaminated.

Problem 4

The people have used so much water that there is hardly any left on earth. When they go to take a shower, water only dribbles out of their faucets. In some parts of the kingdom it is especially dry, but in one area there is still enough water. In that area people still soak in bathtubs and water their lawns by the hour. How should the king try to balance this situation so that it's more fair?

Possible Solutions: The King could invite people from all areas of the kingdom to get together and come up with ideas. As a result, he might limit the use of water everywhere.

Perhaps water could be transported from the area that has water to the areas that do not.

The King could educate his people about the value and importance of water as a resource.

Laws could be passed encouraging people to conserve water. Additional taxes could be imposed on people who use too much water.

Problem 5

In one part of the kingdom there is a rainforest. It has been growing for thousands of years, and every imaginable tree, bird, mammal and insect lives there. About 10 years ago a company decided to cut down the trees because it could make a large profit. There was great demand for the rainforest wood, because people liked to make houses and furniture from it. Now half of the rainforest is gone.

A family who lives nearby is concerned that so many trees are disappearing. They realize that our earth can only stay healthy when forests are allowed to live, and especially rainforests. They complained to the company, but the company told them to get lost. "If we stop cutting down the trees, our company will go out of business and a lot of people will lose their jobs," the president said. Should the king listen to the company or the family? And what should he do?

Possible Solutions: The King could point out to the company that forests are the habitat for living creatures. Forests use carbon dioxide for growth and give off oxygen, which people need. Rainforests are special because they contain the secrets to many of our medical problems. If we cut them down, we might be missing out on cures that could save people's lives.

TV ads could be used that discouraged people from buying rainforest wood. This would reduce the demand for it, and the company would find out that few people wanted to buy it anymore. Once there was less money to be made, the company might decide to stop cutting down rainforest trees.

The King could also ban cutting down rainforest trees. That would force the company to move to another area that wasn't quite as critical.

And, of course, the King could make sure that the company replanted trees every time it cut them down.

24

RIDDLES

Background

Most children enjoy riddles. You have probably noticed how much they like tricking you with clever riddles. Here's a chance to try some that are related to the environment. You may choose to ask these riddles of your child or let her pose them to you. Whichever way you go, remember: No peeking at the answers until you've tried to guess each one! When your child is through with them, see if she can come up with at least three riddles of her own.

The Goal

To reinforce your child's concern for the earth through a variety of riddles.

Age Range

6 - 10 years

Materials Needed

Pencil and paper.

Riddle No. 1: I'm made of many flavors and when I get hot I blow bubbles. What am I?

Riddle No. 2: What is trapped in the dark under a lot of pressure, can only escape when someone pushes its head down, and once free, flies away to eat up the sky?

Riddle No. 3: If I'm lucky I will live many times. I'm tough enough to survive getting flattened every time I die. When I come back to life, I have a new shape and color. What am I?

Riddle No. 4: What is invisible when it's clean and visible when it's dirty?

Riddle No. 5: What's green and eats Peanut M&Ms?

Riddle No. 6: The lazier you are, the fatter I get and the worse I smell. What am I?

Riddle No. 7: What kind of water likes cars?

Riddle No. 8: When is the only time you can arrest your mother and not get in trouble?

Riddle No. 9: The stingier you are with me, the better I like it. What am I?

Riddle No. 10: What kind of bank runs out of money the more people use it?

NOW LET YOUR CHILD TRY SOME!

Answers to Riddles

1. Garden Fresh Soup
2. CFCs in an aerosol can
3. An aluminum can
4. The air
5. The Friendly Green Ghost
6. A landfill
7. A car pool
8. When you're the Ecology Cop
9. Ground water
10. The Earth Bank

25

SONGS

Background

Music is an excellent way to reinforce earth friendly practices. The song on the following page personalizes a child's concern for the earth. Go through the words of the song with your child so that he is familiar with them. If either of you plays an instrument, feel free to accompany yourselves.

When you're through singing the song, help your child create additional verses or write your own music. It's a good idea to write the lyrics first, and then set them to a melody. If you like, write lyrics to a popular tune and sing them.

The Goal

To reinforce your child's commitment to the environment through music.

Age Range

4 - 10 years

Materials Needed

Song (see next page), paper and pencil, a basic knowledge of music, and a musical instrument (optional).

I LOVE THE EARTH

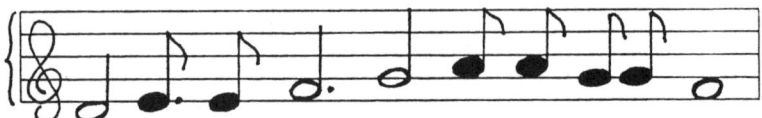

I love the earth, and all its living things

I will care for it, I will care for it,

Un - til my dy - ing day. Every chance I get

I'll pro - tect it, and show o - thers the way

I'll   be   hea - lthy,   I'll   be   hap - py

And   so   will   the   earth.

26

BIRD BUDDIES

Background

In winter birds often need food and water. Cold weather freezes their sources of drinking water, and seeds are buried beneath the snow. Helping wild animals survive is an earth friendly thing to do. With very little effort, you and your child can turn your yard into a haven for birds and other small animals.

See if you and your child can identify several species of birds in your vicinity. Your encyclopedia or a book from the library should provide basic information. Are there other animals you catch a glimpse of from time to time, such as squirrels or chipmunks? They will be interested in your seeds, too.

The Goal

To become a "Bird Buddy" by setting one or more bird feeders outside and supplying birds with fresh water.

Age Range

4 - 12 years

Materials Needed

Bird seed, bird houses (optional), a bucket that is heated, water.

ACTIVITY 1

Fill a bird feeder with seeds. Put it on your deck or some other place where it is visible from the window. Go inside and wait. How long does it take the birds to discover it?

ACTIVITY 2

Fill your bucket with water. Set it close to the bird feeder. If it's winter time, it should be close enough to an electrical outlet that you can plug it in to keep the water from freezing.

ACTIVITY 3

Spend time with your child watching the birds. Observe their behavior and remark on it. Is one bird more pushy than the rest? Do some prefer eating from the ground instead of the feeder? Perhaps other wildlife has noticed your backyard refuge and is attracted to it. Watch out for predators such as owls. You'll notice a flurry of activity if one comes too close. Make sure your child remembers that part of being a "Bird Buddy" is to replenish the supply of seeds and water on a regular basis.

27

EARTH-DAY PARTY!

Background

Talk to your child about birthdays. He probably knows when his is, but ask him if he knows when the earth's birthday is. No one really knows. However, in 1970 people all over the United States declared April 22 as Earth Day, and this was celebrated again in 1990. Perhaps April 22 would be a good day to have an Earth-Day Party, or some day close to it. However, any day you decide upon is fine.

Once you have decided on the date, sit down with your child and make a list of the friends he would like to invite. Give them at least 10-14 days' notice. Tell them what kind of party it is, and ask them to bring one wrapped present that is earth friendly. (Earth friendly might simply mean a toy that is sturdy enough to last many years, not wear out after a few uses.) You might want to consider a price limit of $10 per present, or any other limit you feel comfortable with.

Discuss some of the things you would like to have or do at your child's Earth-Day Party. Some ideas are:

- A cake with green frosting and green candles, and lime ice cream
- Green streamers decorating the house
- Green paper squares hidden around the living room (for the game)
- Green juice
- A basketball wrapped in green paper to represent the earth (or a globe)
- Music

Review the activities in this chapter and select the ones you would like to include in your Earth-Day Party. You may think of some other activities, too.

Let's Celebrate!

The Goal

To influence your child's friends to be earth friendly, too. What better way than with a party?

Age Range

4 - 7 years

Materials Needed

Cake and frosting, green food coloring, black frosting (optional), Lemon-Lime Gatorade or other green drink, 50 1-inch squares of green paper, green streamers (optional), 1 earth friendly present, green candles, green napkins, green cloth tablecloth, plates, cups, silverware, a basketball or globe, 1 sheet of green wrapping paper, scotch tape, black marker, lime ice cream, matches, three small glasses, scissors, ice cream scooper, knife, music, 5-7 of your child's friends.

ACTIVITY 1

Let your child assist you in making the cake. After it has cooled, add green food coloring to the frosting and spread it around on the cake. If you wish, write "Happy Earth-Day" on it in black frosting. Add as many candles as you want. Perhaps each candle could represent 1 billion years.

ACTIVITY 2

If you're not using a globe, ask your child to wrap the basket-ball in green paper and draw a smiley face on it. Set the basketball or globe on your table and wedge it in place with three small glasses that are upside-down.

ACTIVITY 3

Buy a present that you consider earth friendly and ask your child to wrap it. Set it next to your basketball earth or globe.

ACTIVITY 4

With your child's help, decorate at least one room of your house with the green streamers.

ACTIVITY 5

Assist your child to cut up 50 squares of green paper. Then hide them around the living room in places that children will be able to discover. If you have breakable vases nearby, be sure to secure or move them.

ACTIVITY 6

Before your child's friends arrive, set the table with plates, silverware, and the cake.

ACTIVITY 7

As the children arrive, ask them to place their gifts by the "earth" on the table. Your child can help you, or you might prefer to do this yourself.

ACTIVITY 8

When everyone is there, tell them it's time to play a game. Explain that there are 50 squares of green paper hidden around the living room, and show them what one looks like. Tell them that when you say, "Go," they are to find as many as they can. Later on the winner will be able to select the first present, the child with the second highest number of squares will be able to select the second present, and so on. (Since your child helped you hide the squares, he won't be able to play or give hints. He'll take the last present. Make sure he understands that this is good manners, and that the last present may turn out to be the best, anyway.)

Give the children about 5 minutes for the game. Then stop them, ask them to count their squares, and write their names and number of squares on a sheet of paper.

ACTIVITY 9

Ask the children to gather around the table. It's time to sing "Happy Earth-Day" to the earth. If you're musically inclined, you might like to teach them the words to "I Love the Earth" and sing that too.

ACTIVITY 10

Cut the cake and put one scoop of ice cream on each plate. Pour one cup of Gatorade for each child. Hopefully they can eat and drink this sitting around the table.

ACTIVITY 11

When the children are through eating, clear the table and ask them to wash their hands. Then it's time for the winner to select his present. Let him open it while everyone watches. Then go down the line, until you end with your child.

ACTIVITY 12

After all the presents are open, ask the children to remove the scotch tape and bows from their wrapping paper, fold it, and put it in the place where you collect recyclable paper.

ACTIVITY 13

Talk about the presents. What is earth friendly about each of them? What kinds of things can the children do in their own homes to be more earth friendly?

ACTIVITY 14

As the children leave, thank them for helping the earth celebrate its birthday.

Hint: If it's possible to talk your spouse or a friend into helping you with the Earth-Day Party, it will be much easier to manage the children and activities. You probably already thought of that, didn't you?

28

ZOAB THE ZOMBIE

Background

Americans throw away 154 million tons of garbage every year. About half of this is recyclable, including tin cans, plastic bottles, milk cartons, and cardboard. Is your child learning to recycle any of these items in addition to the other products you normally recycle? Check with your local recycling center to see what kinds of items they will accept. They may have some requirements, such as removing the labels from soup cans or separating white from colored paper before you take it to them. Recycling everything you can will greatly reduce the amount of garbage that ends up at your landfill.

Explain to your child that there are other kinds of materials that should never be taken to a landfill. For example, products such as car batteries, air conditioners or refrigerators should always be taken to an agency that specializes in treating or recycling hazardous wastes. The CFCs in products with air conditioning are extremely harmful to the environment.

Ask her if she would like to see a landfill, and then later hear a story about one landfill that turned into a monster. Warn her in advance that it's a science fiction story with no ending. She'll have to decide what happens.

The Goal

To familiarize your child with a landfill; and through creative story-telling to arrive at a solution to the landfill monster, "Zoab the Zombie."

Age Range

6 - 9 years

Materials Needed

Access to the landfill closest to your home, transportation, and the following story.

ACTIVITY 1

Call the office that oversees your local landfill (probably a government service). Ask if it would be possible for you to drive there and let your child see it. Be prepared for restrictions on when you can go and where you can stand. You may only be able to get as close as the outside gate. Take your child there on a Saturday afternoon and let her observe it. What does she see? Are there bulldozers at work? Seagulls circling overhead? How does it smell? Perhaps she can identify garbage that should have been recycled. Talk about it on the way home.

ACTIVITY 2

Read "Zoab the Zombie" to your child, preferably after she has seen the landfill.

ZOAB THE ZOMBIE

Greenville was a beautiful place to live. It had lots of nice homes and playgrounds, and along each road there was a bike path for kids to use. When visitors came to Greenville, they were impressed with the clean streets and fresh air.

No one paid any attention to the landfill. After all, it was five miles away from the town. It was hidden behind a hill, and a high fence kept everyone away. Unless you wandered too close, you couldn't see it or smell it.

For several years the landfill had been getting fuller and fuller. People dumped hazardous wastes into it when they should have known better. Refrigerators and cars and old batteries were mixed in with other trash. The landfill turned into a frightful mess. Even when it grew taller than the hill, no one paid any attention. They just kept piling up the trash higher and higher.

One night there was a terrible storm. Thunder boomed and flashes of lightning struck the earth. One of the bolts of lightning touched the landfill, and something strange began to happen. Blue light crackled around thousands of batteries, and it spread over the landfill like a network of veins.

Then there was a rumble, like a belch coming from the guts of the earth. Parts of the landfill moved. First it was a long line that began to lift up. And then another, like two legs. An arm popped up and began to claw at the sky. Its fingers were made of refrigerators. With a mighty roar, a head sat up and looked around.

"I'M HUNGRY!" it boomed. It grabbed several cars and ate them, crunching into the bolts and metal like they were candy. It sucked the acid out of batteries and licked its lips. When it was full, it decided to stand. The ground shifted like a fearsome earthquake as the monster stumbled to its feet. Old phone books and messy disposable diapers fell from its body.

"ZO-AAAA-BBB," it said. It smashed the fence to the landfill on its way out. Its legs covered a mile with every step it took.

The people of Greenville had no warning. One minute they were peacefully minding their business and the next a zombie appeared out of no where. It gobbled up their cars and ripped the roofs off their homes. It didn't eat people, but it grabbed their refrigerators and devoured them.

"ZO-AAAA-BBB!" it roared. It thundered through the town, flattening buildings and anything else in its path. People ran shrieking out into the streets.

"Help!" they cried. "Save us from Zoab the Zombie!"

The police decided to head off the beast from the other side of town. They aimed their guns at its chest and fired. Some bullets struck the wall of cars on its belly and others sank into its tires and barrels. Zoab caught a few bullets and ate them.

"MORE!" he growled. "ZO-AAAA-BBB WANTS MORE!"

"Oh, no!" the police gasped. "What are we going to do? We've created a monster!"

"It's our landfill come to life!" another said, trembling. "Do you think we should get some dynamite and blow it up?"

"That would just scatter it all over the country," the first policeman said. "It would kill more people by falling out of the sky in pieces than by walking around."

"Then what should we do?" the other policemen wailed. "It's coming closer!"

"Fire! Let's set it on fire!" someone shouted.

"Then it will burn us all down!" the first policeman said.

"We've got to use our heads."

"In another minute we won't have any!" someone snapped. "We've got to do something right now!"

What did they do?

Some ideas are:

- What about helicopters that fly around Zoab the Zombie with giant magnets suspended from them? The magnets could pull the batteries and refrigerators away from Zoab's body. Once enough of them had been removed, Zoab wouldn't have a source of energy to keep going. It would lose power and fall over.

- What about a time machine? A child could fly back in time to when the landfill was first being used. She could refuse to allow anything with CFCs to be dumped there. That way Zoab the Zombie couldn't have formed in the first place. When she returns to the present, Zoab would fade away.

29

ON OUR WAY

Background

Explain to your child that there are many places where people dispose of their garbage. Some garbage will certainly end up at the landfill. But our best alternative is to recycle as many products as possible so that less will have to be buried in the earth.

The object of the maze in this chapter is to find the best place for your recyclable garbage. There are several destinations; your child's job is to end up at the best one. You may wish to photocopy the maze at 140% and let him mark up the copy.

The Goal

To reinforce your child's habit of taking recyclable garbage to a recycling center, through use of a simple maze.

Age Range

4 - 7 years

Materials Needed

Pencil and maze (see next page).

ACTIVITY 1

Ask your child to draw a line through the maze to the best destination. Ask him why it's the best. What's wrong with taking bottles and aluminum cans to a landfill?

TRASH!

Can you find the best destination?

HIGHWAY

LANDFILL

OCEAN

BACKYARD

RECYCLE CENTER

ACTIVITY 2

Can your child create his own environmental maze? He might wish to include several destinations, including one "best" one. It's up to him. Encourage him to be creative.

30

BUG BUSTERS

Background

Most of us do not like bugs in our homes. Bugs are such insects as flies, cockroaches, beetles, mosquitoes, ants, bees, termites or spiders. When we think our home is being invaded by them, we often choose the most toxic (or deadly) pest control method first. Often a less toxic approach would have the desired effect, with far fewer risks to our health.

Tell your child that bugs may be earth friendly, even though we don't like some of them. For example, bees sting but they are necessary to pollinate flowers.

Bugs can be unfriendly, too. Termites eat wood and can cause structural damage in our homes. Mosquitoes can spread diseases such as malaria.

The most earth friendly way to combat indoor bugs is with an approach called Integrated Pest Management (IPM). This involves checking out the lifestyle and environment of the bug and disrupting its habitat. If chemicals are needed, they should be used wisely and at the most vulnerable period of the bug's life.

Review the following steps on Integrated Pest Management with your child. It will help you develop a plan for dealing with an indoor bug problem.

INTEGRATED PEST MANAGEMENT STEPS

• Be on the alert for bug problems before they get out of control.

• How bad is the problem? Do you really need to take action, or can you tolerate some inconvenience?

- Identify the specific kind of bug in your house. For example, there are four major kinds of cockroaches, not just one. Different kinds of stinging bees include wasps, hornets, honeybees, etc.

- Find out all you can about the life cycle of the bug, where it likes to hide, what it likes to eat, and where it mates.

- If roaches are the problem, try spinkling boric acid in areas where they travel or hide. After they ingest it they'll die within a week or two.

- Disrupt or get rid of the places where the bugs enter your home. Caulking cracks in your home is a good way to keep them out.

- Get rid of the food or water that attracts bugs. Thoroughly clean your kitchen after each use and promptly dispose of trash.

- Try non-toxic traps next, if you need reinforcements in your battle. These "roach motels" are most effective when placed along the edges of walls or in dark enclosed places.

- Your last resort should be chemical control. Bug bombs and poisonous chemical sprays can be dangerous. Use them only when absolutely necessary, and with extreme caution.

Explain to your child that when you use chemicals, they may have an impact on other species. For example, your dog might lick up boric acid meant for bugs and die. That's why it's important to be very careful about using poisonous chemicals. You wouldn't want other species such as birds or cats to get sick from them.

After you and your child have studied the indoor bug problem and decided upon an appropriate approach for your home, you're ready for one or more of the activities in this chapter.

Recommended Reading: Information on Integrated Pest Management in the home is available at the Bio Integral Resource Center, P.O. Box 7414, Berkeley, CA 94707. Include $1 for postage, and ask for a copy of the 12-page pamphlet entitled "Least-Toxic Pest Management Publications Catalogue."

The Goal
To encourage your child to be a "Bug Buster" who uses Integrated Pest Management to control indoor bugs.

Age Range
8 - 12 years

Materials Needed
Encyclopedia or information regarding pests and pest control, caulker and caulking, boric acid, non-toxic traps.

ACTIVITY 1

BORIC ACID BUG BUSTER. Make sure your child understands that boric acid is poisonous. Because it is, we recommend that you handle it. Explain that she should *never* eat any, and it should always be kept away from pets.

Your child can be of assistance in helping you reach out-of-the-way spots or assuring that the areas you sprinkle are inaccessible to your pets. When you are through, replace the boric acid in a safe place. Wash your hands thoroughly.

ACTIVITY 2

CAULKING ASSISTANT. Fill your caulking gun while your child watches. Then let her accompany you around the house as you plug holes. If she is old enough, let her help caulk a few holes.

ACTIVITY 3

THE SUPER-DUPER INSPECTOR. Ask your child to help inspect the kitchen after each use. She might be assigned a specific duty, such as scouting for stray crumbs on the counters or floor, and then helping you clean them up. Or she might keep an eye out for bugs in cupboards or cannisters.

ACTIVITY 4

THE DETECTIVE. Ask your child to help you monitor the bug problem. How many bugs were there before you started your Integrated Pest Management program? How many were there after two weeks? A month? Do you feel that you've brought them under control?

31

THE CHAMP:
An Interview

Background

Explain to your child that you'd like to play a puppet game
with him. He will pretend to be "The Champ" who has
received a Green Globe award for his earth friendly activities.
You will be the interviewer, getting an interview with him for
the six o'clock news. Your interview will focus on what he has
done to deserve the Green Globe award.

The Goal

To reinforce your child's pride in his earth friendly activities
through an interview format.

Age Range

5 - 8 years

Materials Needed

A pair of socks, a toothpick, an olive (preferably black), a
green marble (or other small object, such as a small rubber
ball).

Before You Start

Poke the toothpick through the bottom of the olive so that it
looks like a microphone. Both you and your child need to pull
a sock over one hand. As the interviewer puppet, you should
control the microphone. When your child talks, place it close
to his puppet's "mouth." Your child's puppet should be
holding his Green Globe award (the marble or ball).

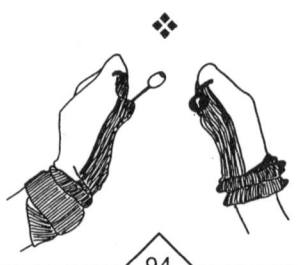

VARIATION 1

The basic interview:

YOU: Are you ready, Champ?

CHAMP: Yes.

YOU: Tell me, Champ, what kinds of things did you do
         to deserve this award?

CHAMP: Well, I recycle pop cans and newspapers, and I
         turn off the lights when I'm not using them, and I
         don't use any more water than I have to... [and
         any other earth friendly things he does]

YOU: Wow! That's pretty impressive. I imagine it's hard
         to remember to do all that.

CHAMP: No, it's not! It's easy.

YOU: What advice do you have for people who are not
         earth friendly?

CHAMP: I say to them: Don't be stupid! Don't be lazy! Get
         up off your butt and start taking care of the earth,
         or it won't be around when we grow up.

YOU: That's pretty straight advice, Champ.

CHAMP: I'm that kind of kid.

YOU: Well, thank you, Champ. Before we close, is there
         anyone you would like to thank for helping you
         win the Green Globe Award?

CHAMP: My parents. They're the greatest!

YOU: I agree. And there you have it, folks. An interview
         with The Champ himself. He's a very smart kid,
         wouldn't you say?

VARIATION 2

Your child changes places with you and becomes the interviewer. He gets to control the microphone and ask the questions.

CHAMP: Are you ready, Mrs. Goose?

YOU: Yes.

CHAMP: Tell me, Mrs. Goose, what kinds of things do you do to be earth friendly?

YOU: Well, I use a non-aerosol hair spray, and I take paper bags with me to the store when I shop, and I ride my bicycle whenever possible instead of the car. . . [and anything else]

CHAMP: I'm impressed. But why, if you do all these things, did your kid win the Green Globe award instead of you?

YOU: I'm not sure. [Begins to cry] I try so hard to be earth friendly, but I guess that kid of mine is even friendlier.

CHAMP: Well, that's a tough break for you, Mrs. Goose. But remember, there's always next year. Maybe your kid will mess up and you'll be the new winner.

YOU: I don't think so. My kid is pretty smart. You see, he learned how to be earth friendly when he was little. I didn't learn until I was older, and so it's a lot harder to break my old habits.

CHAMP: My advice to you is: Keep trying! Hang in there! And I'll be around to talk to you next year. In the meantime, Mrs. Goose, good luck.

YOU: Thanks.

VARIATION 3

Make up your own themes and variations. There's no limit, so long as you use your imagination. If you wish to be more creative with your sock puppets, or have other puppets on hand, go for it! Keep it fun and geared to your child's attention span.

32

HOW DOES IT FEEL?

Background

Ask your child to imagine that she is the earth. Tell her that she will need to shut her eyes as you describe situations to her. She should tell you how she feels after each description.

The Goal

To increase your child's awareness of how the earth "feels" when people are unfriendly to it, and when they are friendly to it.

Age Range

3 - 7 years

Materials Needed

None

SITUATION 1

The sun is shining on your bright purple flowers, and a ladybug lights on one of your petals. Its little body tickles your skin. HOW DOES IT FEEL?

SITUATION 2

A man dumps a huge barrel of acid into your clear blue stream. It's red and gooey and stinks really bad. HOW DOES IT FEEL?

SITUATION 3

You only have a little bit of water left in your stomach. A bunch of pipes are stuck into you like straws, and people are sucking and sucking on the water. When the pipes don't bring up enough water, the people suck harder and the pressure gets worse. HOW DOES IT FEEL?

SITUATION 4

A city council decides to turn several acres into a park. The park has a pond where ducks like to swim. Yesterday a mother duck taught her babies to swim behind her in the water. As they paddled around, the water swished against your skin in little circles. HOW DOES IT FEEL?

SITUATION 5

Your air used to smell sweet and clean. Now millions of cars spew out fumes all day long. The smelly carbon monoxide leaves black dust all over your face and nose, and when you try to breathe your nostrils get clogged up. HOW DOES IT FEEL?

SITUATION 6

Bulldozers push sharp metal objects into your stomach. Garbage crushes your chest and stinky disposable diapers are flattened against your skin. Cockroaches and beetles crawl around looking for food. Just when you think you can't stand any more pressure, another dumptruck unloads its trash on you. HOW DOES IT FEEL?

SITUATION 7

A small girl plants a tree. It grows bright green leaves that provide shade from the sun during hot afternoons. When the wind blows, its roots tug lightly at your chest. HOW DOES IT FEEL?

33

WATER COLORING

Background

In environmental science, various colors represent the condition of water. Explain to your child that the following colors have these meanings:

Blue = Clean
Green = Clean, but with plant life
Red = Alarm: indicates industrial discharges
Black = Potentially contaminated

Make sure your child knows that "industrial discharge" is the water that a factory gets rid of after it uses it. This wastewater may be treated or untreated, and it may be contaminated with chemicals. He should also know that "contaminated" means dirty or polluted.

Now ask him if he's like to draw some pictures using these water colors.

The Goal

To increase your child's understanding of these colors in relation to the environment through a simple coloring exercise.

Age Range

4 - 7 years

Materials Needed

Water colors or crayons, pencil and paper.

❖

ACTIVITY 1

Ask your child to draw the following objects on his sheet of paper:

- A house with a pond in the backyard
- A factory with smoke coming out of its chimney
- The factory pumping industrial discharge into a river
- A lake downstream of the factory

ACTIVITY 2

Now ask your child to color the objects he has drawn, using blue, green, red, and black to indicate the condition of the water.

When he has finished, point to each body of water. Ask him what condition it is in, and why.

34

T-SHIRT ART

Background

Ask your child if she would like to design and make an earth friendly T-shirt. She can create it herself (with a little assistance from you) and then wear it whenever she likes. A weekend afternoon might be an ideal time for this activity.

The Goal

To reinforce your child's earth friendly attitude through a T-shirt that she designs and wears.

Age Range

5 - 10 years

Materials Needed

Paper, pencil, a plain T-shirt, indelible marker(s), scraps of green cloth and/or other colors, scissors, pins, needle and thread or sewing machine or iron-on fabric bond and iron.

❖

ACTIVITY 1

Ask your child to sketch an earth friendly design for her T-shirt using pencil and paper. It may be as simple or complex as she wishes. Bring out any materials you have on hand to assist her in planning her design.

Hint: A simple design idea might include large letters that say "EARTH FRIENDLY" on the upper part of the T-shirt, and a green circle with a smiley face on it directly beneath the letters.

When your child has finished her design, review it with her. Does she plan to use her marker for letters or cut out individual letters from cloth? Does she want to cut out objects from your scraps of cloth and sew (or bond) them to the T-shirt, or draw directly on the T-shirt with different colors of markers?

Hint: Check to see whether the markers bleed through the fabric. Your child may have to slip a newspaper in between the T-shirt if she uses a marker to write on the front.

If your child wants to cut out an object from a scrap of cloth, help her pencil the outline on the cloth before she cuts it. Let her arrange the pieces on the T-shirt and help pin them in place. Then you're ready to attach the objects to the T-shirt using your preferred method.

ACTIVITY 2

When the T-shirt is completed, encourage your child to wear it to the movies or anywhere else she feels comfortable. If you both think it's good enough, enter it in your local fair. Who knows—it might win a ribbon!

35

THE GREAT DIAPER EXPERIMENT

Background

As we noted earlier, disposable diapers can take up to 500 years to decompose vs. 1-6 months for cloth diapers.

Ask your child if he knows what the word "BIODEGRAD-ABLE" means. It's a big one, so repeat it with him. Ask him to look up the definition and write it on a sheet of paper. It will be similar to this:

"Something that is capable of being decomposed, especially by bacterial action."

Does your child know what "decomposed" means? If not, look that up too. Most children will know what "to become rotten or decay" means. Perhaps your child has seen the remains of an animal in the woods, or a piece of fruit (such as a strawberry) that went bad and had to be thrown out. Can he think of other examples of things that decayed?

Make sure he knows that bacteria are very tiny plants that can do useful things, like decompose dead leaves and trees so they're returned to the earth. (Bacteria are also called microbes, or microorganisms.) They're so small that you can only see them with the help of a microscope. These bacteria use dead products as a source of food and nutrients.

Biodegradable is a relative term. Most organic, or carbon-based, matter is biodegradable, including cloth and plastic. However, plastic is relatively non-biodegradable because it takes so much longer than cloth to degrade. Plastic is also dependent on other factors to degrade, such as adequate moisture or nutrients.

Ask your child if he would like to try an experiment. Show him two diapers, one disposable and the other cloth. Ask him which one he thinks is biodegradable within a year or less. He may choose the cloth diaper, or he may think both are biodegradable in that timeframe. There's an easy way to find out: bury both of them in your backyard, leave them for several months, up to a year. Then dig them up and see what's left. Ask your child if he'd like to try this experiment.

The Goal

To teach your child the concept "BIODEGRADABLE" in a hands-on experiment.

Age Range

5 - 9 years

Materials Needed

One disposable diaper (not soiled), one cloth diaper (also not soiled), shovel, two wood stakes, hammer, small area in backyard, pencil and paper, dictionary.

ACTIVITY 1

You and your child need to carry both diapers, the shovel, markers and hammer into your backyard. Dig two holes at least one foot deep, and at least two feet away from each other. Bury the disposable diaper in one hole and cover it with dirt. Use the hammer to pound a marker over it and clearly mark it "Disposable." Then bury your cloth diaper in the second hole, cover it and mark it "Cloth."

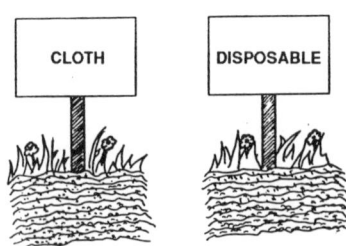

When you go back inside, mark today's date on your calendar. A good time of year to begin this experiment is the spring. Count six months (or up to one year) from today's date on your calendar and mark it too.

ACTIVITY 2

Periodically during the six months' or more wait to dig up the diapers, refresh your child's memory about the experiment and ask him to speculate on how the diapers are faring. Does he think they are being attacked by bacteria or bugs? Pique his curiosity, but don't let him dig up the diapers! Increase his anticipation with remarks like, "Only two more months until Dig Up Day," or "only ten more days to go."

ACTIVITY 3

Six months after the day of burial, return to your two marked graves with your child. Assist him to dig up the disposable diaper first. What condition is it in? Has any part of it decomposed?

Now help him dig up the cloth diaper. What condition is it in? Has any part of it decomposed? Is any of it still recognizeable?

When you return inside, ask your child to write down his observations about both diapers. Were the disposable diapers biodegradable within the six-month timeframe? Or were the cloth diapers? What conclusions can he draw from this experiment?

36

MR. GRABOLA
AND MR. NIPPIT

Background

In 1968 Garrett Hardin published *The Tragedy of the Commons*. In it he said that the major obstacle to solving problems like pollution and overpopulation is the conflict between the short-term welfare of individuals and the long-term welfare of society.

To illustrate this problem, he used the example of the commons. In Europe and America common grazing lands used to be available to everyone in the village. Since the commons were free, it was to each individual's benefit to graze as many cattle on the common grass area as he could. However, when each person did what was best for himself, there was not enough grass for everyone and the commons were destroyed.

This tragedy carries over into many environmental issues. For example, one way people used to increase their wealth and influence was by having large families. This was best for them, but it had a serious impact on society. In the interest of survival, we must learn to enlarge our thinking from the selfish to the societal.

Pose a situation to your child. What if she could have anything she wanted? What would it be? For example, let's say she says "toys." In your hypothetical example, give her all the toys she wants. They wouldn't fit into your house, so you'd have to buy a bigger house. Then you'd have to find another job to earn more money to buy more toys. Finally, after taking out too many loans and not being able to make the payments, you go bankrupt. You and your family lose the house and all your child's toys. Now your family has nothing. Was the unlimited supply of toys for one child in the best interest of the whole family?

Discuss the dilemma of selfish interests vs. family interests. Now your child is ready for the story of Mr. Grabola and Mr. Nippit. At the conclusion of the story, ask your child which person was *really* smarter.

The Goal
To increase your child's awareness of the consequences of selfish vs. societal lifestyles, through a story of two people: Mr. Grabola and Mr. Nippit.

Age Range
6 - 10 years

Materials Needed
None

MR. GRABOLA AND MR. NIPPIT

Once upon a time there were two men who lived in Meadow Park. Mr. Grabola and his wife built a huge farmhouse in one area of town, and Mr. Nippit and his wife owned a rather small, modest home next door.

In the middle of Meadow Park there was a field that was commonly owned by the town. Anyone could bring their cows to this area and let them feed on the grass. It was free, so long as the people lived within the city limits of Meadow Park.

Mr. Grabola decided that since the food for his cows was free, he was going to make a lot of money. He bought 100 cows, more than anyone else in town, and let them graze in the common area.

"Boy, am I smart," he chuckled. "I'm going to make so much cashola from my cows' milk that I'll be rich in no time." As he rubbed his hands together, another thought crossed his mind. If he had ten or twelve children, they could milk all the cows and save even more money. Then he wouldn't have to hire workers to help him.

Each year Mr. Grabola and his wife had a new child. And as the children grew up, he assigned daily chores to them. The older ones were in charge of herding the cows to and from the common area, and the younger ones milked cows like crazy in the morning and at night.

The cash from Mr. Grabola's milk sales mounted. He was extremely pleased with himself. Soon he found that his house wasn't big enough anymore, so he built himself an even bigger mansion on his property.

Each morning when Mr. Grabola went to the bank to deposit his money, he passed Mr. Nippit on the way to the common area. Mr. Nippit was thin and tall, and he only owned two cows.

"What an idiot Nippit is," Mr. Grabola said to himself. "He's got all this free food for his cows staring him in the face, and he's too stupid to do anything about it."

One day Mr. Grabola couldn't stand it any more. He stopped Mr. Nippit on the way to the bank. "Do you mind if I ask you a question?" he said.

"Of course not," Mr. Nippit replied.

"Well, why don't you make better use of the commons? You could be a rich man like me if you bought more cows and had more children to milk them. Just look at the size of my house compared to yours. I've got 200 cows, 12 children, 10 cars, and a mansion. And you live right next door in the same small house you've always had, with just two cows and two children. Why don't you wise up and get rich like me?"

Mr. Nippit looked at him and smiled. "Why should I?" he said. "I'm happy the way I am. Besides, if everyone did what you're doing, we wouldn't have a common area. It would be ruined, and then no one would benefit."

Mr. Grabola shook his head. He was disgusted with his neighbor's stupidity. "Suit yourself," he shrugged. "But I think it's pretty dumb not to take advantage of all the free food you can while it lasts."

With a curt nod, Mr. Grabola rushed away to the bank.

Ask your child, who is smarter—Mr. Grabola or Mr. Nippit? Why? What will eventually happen to the common area if Mr. Grabola keeps overusing it?

37

RESOURCES: RENEWABLE vs. NONRENEWABLE

Background

The earth's nonrenewable resources are being used at an alarming rate. Unfortunately, nonrenewable resources can't be replaced. They include such things as coal, oil, and natural gas. At the present time Americans are 96% dependent on nonrenewable sources of energy. As these resources are used up, we must begin to reduce our demand for them. And at the same time we must learn to use renewable resources in a clean and safe manner.

Make sure your child knows the difference between renewable and nonrenewable resources:

Resource: Anything produced naturally that is used by a group of people. Fresh water, oil, and gold are some examples.

Renewable Resources: Natural resources that can last forever because they are produced continuously. For example, when a renewable resource dies it produces seeds so that its offspring will replace it.

Nonrenewable Resources: Natural resources that can be used up completely. There is only a limited supply in the earth, and when they're gone, that's it.

Now ask if she'd like to draw some pictures of renewable and nonrenewable resources in a way that tells them apart.

The Goal

To teach your child to tell the difference between renewable and nonrenewable resources.

Age Range

7 - 10 years

Materials Needed

Paper, crayons, pencil, scissors, paste.

ACTIVITY 1

On a sheet of paper, ask your child to draw the following objects with his crayons:

- a pool of oil
- a tree
- a lump of coal
- water
- a field of corn
- sand
- a shrub
- an aluminum can
- a gold coin
- rain
- a can of gasoline

ACTIVITY 2

Assist your child in cutting out each of these objects from the paper with a scissors.

ACTIVITY 3

On a separate sheet of paper, write the word "RENEWABLE" on the top left hand side, and the word "NONRENEWABLE" on the top right hand side. (If your child has a hard time writing these words, help him.) Divide the paper into two columns.

Now ask your child in which column each of the drawings belongs. Talk to him about each item to help him decide whether it is renewable or nonrenewable. Remember, if there's only a limited supply in the earth and the resource doesn't have the ability to reproduce itself continuously, it's nonrenewable.

Your child's drawings should be in these columns:

RENEWABLE	NONRENEWABLE
Tree	Oil
Water	Coal
Field of corn	Sand
Shrub	Aluminum can
Rain	Gold coin
	Gasoline

When his drawings are in the right column, paste them down. (Scotch tape will work fine, too.) Then post your child's paper in a prominent spot, such as on the refrigerator or in his room. Encourage him to think of other renewable and nonrenewable resources in the next few weeks. He may want to add other drawings later.

Your child may also want to write "CAUTION" or "WARNING" on the nonrenewable side of his paper. This will serve as a reminder that these resources are limited and we need to use them wisely.

38

SUNKEN SUBMARINE

Background

The average toilet uses 5 - 7 gallons of water each time it is flushed. And if your toilet is flushed 8 times a day, you are using 56 gallons of water every day to dispose of waste. This amounts to over 20,000 gallons of water used by one toilet bowl in a year.

Explain to your child that most toilets waste water, but a special sunken submarine can stop it. After she makes the submarine, you will help her put it in the tank of the toilet. There it will displace water so that not as much is used when someone flushes the toilet.

The Goal

To reduce the amount of water used each time you or your child flushes the toilet by at least 20%.

Age Range

5 - 8 years

Materials Needed

Plastic bottle and cap, small stones, pennies and marbles.

ACTIVITY 1

Assist your child to remove the label from the plastic bottle. Fill it with as many "treasures" as your child wishes, from small stones to pennies and marbles (or any other small, heavy objects desired). Add water and tightly close the cap.

ACTIVITY 2

Ask your child to name the submarine. How about the Sunken Santa Maria? The Waterlogged Witch? The Deep Six Treasure Chest? The Shark Bait II?

ACTIVITY 3

Lift the lid of the toilet tank. Then have your child flush the toilet. As the water flows from the tank to the toilet bowl, let your child place her christened submarine in the bottom of the tank. The water will rise up over it, but because the submarine is in the tank, not as much water will be needed. Make sure she sees how it works. Then replace the lid.

Hint: Your child may want to see her submarine from time to time. If she does, tell her you must be the one to remove the lid because it's so heavy. After a period of time her interest will wane, but in the meantime prepare yourself for a few viewings.

Also, it may take a few tries to get the right sized "submarine" for your toilet bowl. If the plastic bottle is too big, it may not allow enough water pressure to build for flushings. And if it's too small, it's not displacing enough water. You'll get it right without much trouble, though, and then you'll feel good about saving water with every flush.

39

THE LAND RANGER

Background

When people cut down large amounts of trees for commercial use, they leave behind land that may be vulnerable. This practice is called deforestation. Not only does it decrease the earth's supply of oxygen, but it can also cause erosion of the land by both wind and water.

Make sure your child understands that erosion is the wearing away of a surface, such as soil. Trees help stop erosion because their roots are attached to the soil.

Some forest practices are more friendly than others. For example, some tree harvesters replant trees after they cut them down.

Remind your child that trees use carbon dioxide to grow. They produce oxygen as a waste product, and that's what we use to breathe.

Now ask your child to pretend he is the Land Ranger. He may put on a hat to signal that he is on duty. His job is to carry out a secret mission for the federal government. Explain that the Feds want to know whether or not to build a new office on land that has vegetation, or on bare land. They have asked the Land Ranger to do an experiment to find out which location is better.

The Goal

To demonstrate to your child the harmful effects of deforestation, through a simple experiment.

Age Range

6 - 9 years

Materials Needed

Shovel, ground, fan, extension cord (if needed), hose with nozzle, (2) 1-foot square plywood scraps, hat.

ACTIVITY 1

Find a spot in your back yard that has weeds between six and 10 inches tall. Dig up 2 one-foot square clumps of ground. Each clump should be about six inches deep. This dirt must be dry for the experiment to work.

When you and your child have these clumps dug up, place them on your plywood scraps. Leave one clump natural. On the other clump, pull out all the weeds by the roots. Make sure the second clump is completely bare.

ACTIVITY 2

Aim the fan at both clumps. Let it run for 5 minutes or more while you and your child observe. Does any dust blow away from the clump with weeds? How about the bare clump? Did the weeds help keep the soil from eroding?

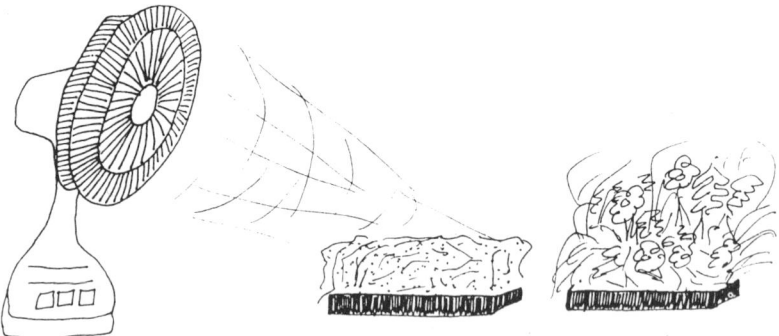

ACTIVITY 3

Now tilt the weeded clump at a 45° angle while your child aims the hose at it. He should be standing and aiming the nozzle directly downward at the clump. Let the water spray for two minutes. What happens to the clump with weeds?

Now spray the bare clump. What happens after two minutes? Does the dirt erode more or less than the clump with weeds?

When you have put away your materials, ask your child to draw conclusions. As the Land Ranger, should he recommend to the Feds that they build their house on land with vegetation or land that is bare? Why?

DEAR LITTLE MISS LANDERS

Background

Ask your child if she knows who Ann Landers is. If she doesn't, read a letter from the Ann Landers column in your newspaper. Explain that Ann gives advice to readers who have problems they can't solve themselves. Ask your child if she would like to be Little Miss Landers and answer some letters from people who don't know what to do about environmental problems. She should sit at the table while you read the letters. After each one, she needs to write her response on her piece of paper. If she isn't sure about what response to make, discuss options with her.

The Goal

To develop your child's environmental problem-solving abilities through a simple exercise.

Age Range

7 - 10 years

Materials Needed

Newspaper, pencil and paper.

❖

Dear Little Miss Landers: I have this nerdy little brother who likes to cook pizzas in the oven. He says they get crispier that way. Anyway, I tried to tell him that the oven uses more energy than the microwave. Many pizzas can be cooked in the microwave these days, so if you can use it instead of the big oven, why not? Besides, the big oven gets our kitchen hotter and it's already hot enough. What should I tell my little twerp of a brother? He won't listen to me, but I know he would listen to you. —Signed, TWERP-SICK.

Possible Answer: The microwave oven does use less energy than big ovens. From that standpoint, it's more earth friendly to use a microwave. But be careful that nothing plugs up the vents on top of the microwave, and never stand close to it while it's on. Some experts warn us not to microwave food on the silver reflective cardboard that comes inside some packages. They say chemicals can be absorbed into the food that way. How about microwaving pizza on a plate?

* * *

Dear Little Miss Landers: My parents have a bunch of old tires sitting around in the back yard. Yesterday I heard them talking about taking them to the dump. I don't think this is a good idea, but I can't think of what else to do. I'm not sure whether these tires are recyclable. What do you recommend? Please hurry and tell me, because Dad wants to take them to the dump tomorrow. —Signed, WHEELER-DEALER, JR.

Possible Answer: It's better to find another use for the tires instead of taking them to the dump. What about using them to landscape part of your yard and planting flowers in the middle? What about giving or selling them to someone else who can use them? What about calling your recycling center to see if they accept tires? It's not a good idea to let old tires lie around because they collect water and mosquitoes can hatch there. If at all possible, find a way to re-use or recycle them.

* * *

Dear Little Miss Landers: Today my mom and I got in an argument when we were shopping. My mom wanted to buy this outrageous dress for me. I mean, it was really cool and everything, but when I looked at the tag it said, "Dry Clean Only." I read somewhere that dry cleaning uses unhealthy chemicals on clothes, and that it's better to buy clothes that can be washed in your washing machine. So I told Mom I would rather buy a dress that didn't have to be dry cleaned. My mom looked at me like I was crazy. So right there, in the middle of the store, we got in an argument. Mom finally said, "FINE! We won't buy you anything, then. How do you like THAT???" We didn't say two words to each other on the ride home. I really do want a new dress, Little Miss Landers, but I want to be earth friendly too. What should I do? —Signed, RAGGEDY ANN II.

Possible Answer: The chemicals used to dry clean clothes can be toxic and they can also pollute the air. Whenever you can buy clothes that are washable, it's more earth friendly than buying clothes that need to be dry cleaned. Perhaps Miss Raggedy Ann II could wait until she and her mother have cooled off to explain this to her. Then later they might look for a dress that didn't have to be dry cleaned.

* * *

Dear Little Miss Landers: I went to the store with my dad yesterday and he made all kinds of "Boo-Boos." You wouldn't believe how many! At any rate, I kept my mouth shut most of the time because Dad was in a really bad mood. But when we got to the refrigerated section, he picked up the kind of cheese that has individually wrapped slices. I know this is wasteful because it uses so much unnecessary plastic. So I stuck it back on the shelf and replaced it with the kind of cheese that isn't sliced. My dad caught me and blew up. He snarled, "Do that again and you'll be sorry, kid!" What can I do about parents like this? —Signed, BAFFLED BRAD.

Possible Answer: Perhaps Brad could wait until his dad is in a better mood. Then he could tell him that the extra plastic used to individually wrap cheese is wasteful and unfriendly to the earth. By cutting the slices ourselves, we reduce the amount of plastic that's used and keep it out of landfills. It may seem like a small step, but it's important.

* * *

Dear Little Miss Landers: Last Christmas my Aunt Maggie gave me a coat that has rabbit fur around the neck. She thought it was a really great present, but I don't like to wear it. For one thing, it means an animal was killed so I could stay warm when there are plenty of other ways to stay warm. And second, I'm afraid another kid is going to splash me with ketchup. I heard some kids talking about it yesterday. My mom won't let me give this coat back to Aunt Maggie, and she says it would be ungrateful to give it to the Salvation Army. But I don't want to wear it, either. Help! What should I do? Please rush your answer before I get splashed. —Signed, DESPER-ATE DIANA.

Possible Answer: Diana is right—she can stay warm by wearing clothes without fur, and that will help keep animals alive. As people become more aware of cruelty to animals, it will be less acceptable to wear fur. If Diana's mother won't allow her to return the coat to her aunt, perhaps she could avoid wearing it. As soon as she outgrows it, she could donate it to a charity.

* * *

Dear Little Miss Landers: My little sister Karen thinks she knows everything. Like, last night when we went to the store she asked Mom if she could pick out the apples. Mom said yes. So Karen goes over to the bin that has these giant, shiny red apples and starts loading them in the bag. I see these other apples that say, "Organically Grown." Sure, the organically grown apples have a few flaws in their skins, but at least they don't have pesticides all over them. Well, I tried to convince Mom to buy the organically grown apples instead. But Karen started to cry and Mom told me to cool it. So now we have apples that look good but aren't as good for you. What should I do? —Signed, THE SMARTER SISTER.

Possible Answer: It is more healthy to buy organically grown apples because they do not have pesticides on them. The Smarter Sister is right. Later she should talk to her mother and explain her

123

reason for wanting to eat organically grown apples. Her mother may have been embarrassed because Karen started to cry in the store. If you and your mom can make decisions about what kind of apples to buy before you go to the store, it will cut down on problems.

* * *

41

TOY GUARDIAN

Background

Discarded toys often end up in landfills and become part of our garbage problem. To prevent this from happening, encourage your child to recycle his toys by passing them along to other children. Of course, the sturdier his toys are when you buy them, the longer they will last.

Ask him if he'd like to become a Toy Guardian by taking better care of his toys and giving old toys to children who want them.

The Goal

To teach your child to be a Toy Guardian who protects his toys from injury and gives them to other children when he outgrows them.

Age Range

3 - 10 years

Materials Needed

Current and old toys.

❖

ACTIVITY 1

Take an inventory of the condition of your child's toys with him. Which ones are in good shape? Praise him for the ones that still look new or are at least usable. Which ones are in poor shape? Ask him to think of ways to protect these damaged toys from further injury. Are any of the damaged toys made of flimsy materials? If so, perhaps these are toys to avoid in the future.

ACTIVITY 2

Sort through your child's toy area with him. Which toys does he no longer use? Ask him to separate the old toys in a pile. Help him bag these unused toys in paper bags.

ACTIVITY 3

Sit down with your child and discuss the bag(s) of unused toys. Who would benefit from them? Are there organizations in your community that serve underprivileged children? Children who are victims of abuse? If so, choose an organization and find out the address. Take your child with you to drop off the toys. Make sure he feels good about donating his toys. Describe how delighted another child will feel when he sees them, especially if that child doesn't have any other toys to play with.

Also emphasize that this activity is a form of recycling. It means your child's old toys won't end up at the landfill, and it's an earth friendly thing to do!

42

LAUNDROMAT STAR

Background

We use much more energy in the laundry room than we realize. We heat water, use more water than necessary, and use electricity to dry our clothes. In addition, many of us also use detergents with phosphates, which can be harmful to the environment.

Phosphates are chemicals that make plants grow faster. At first this may seem friendly, but when the plants die they use oxygen as they decompose. The lack of oxygen hurts fish and other living things. That's why we check the ingredients on boxes of detergent to make sure they don't contain phosphates.

Ask your child if she remembers what "biodegradable" means from the diaper experiment in Chapter 35. (A biodegradable material is something that can be decomposed by bacterial action.)

Be sure you have a phosphate-free, biodegradable detergent in the house before you start the activities in this chapter. If your store doesn't carry a phosphate-free brand, ask them to begin carrying one.

Ask your child if she'd like to become a Laundromat Star who uses earth friendly practices in the laundry room. She would need to learn a few points to save energy and use earth friendly detergent.

The Goal

To teach your child to be a Laundromat Star by using four earth friendly practices in the laundry room.

Age Range

6 - 9 years

Materials Needed

Phosphate-free, biodegradable detergent, clothes line and clothes pins.

ACTIVITY 1

Invite your child to watch you do a load of laundry. Call her attention to the following points of earth friendly laundromat behavior:

1. Set the dial on the washer to "Warm Wash" and "Cold Rinse." This saves energy because not as much warm water is used. If possible, use "Cold Wash" too.

2. Adjust the water level on the washer to the lowest effective setting. This saves water.

3. Use a phosphate-free, biodegradable detergent.

4. When clothes are washed, hang as many of them as possible on a clothes line. This saves electricity.

Ask your child to assist you with these activities.

ACTIVITY 2

Now it's your child's turn. Ask her to wash and dry a load of clothes using the proper laundromat behavior. Observe and assist her wherever possible, and let her explain how her actions are earth friendly. If she misses a point, ask a question to remind her. When she's finished, praise her for becoming a Laundromat Star.

43

THE JOHNNIE GARDEN

Background

Food that we buy from stores may contain residues of dangerous pesticides. This food also takes a great deal of energy to
produce, including gas for farm machinery. To ensure that the
food we eat is earth friendly, we can either grow it ourselves
or buy organically grown products. If you have the ability to
plant a garden close to your house, it is a great experience for
both you and your child.

Talk to your child about which kinds of vegetables he would
like to grow. It's best to start simple and small, perhaps
choosing three vegetables. Some suggestions: carrots, potatoes, peas, radishes, lettuce. Take into consideration how
hardy and disease-resistant these vegetables are so that your
pest control will be easier.

The Goal

To teach your child to plant, tend and harvest a small food
garden, which he has named after himself.

Age Range

5 - 10 years

Materials Needed

Small garden plot, garden tools, seeds, hose or water bucket.

ACTIVITY 1

After you and your child have decided which vegetables to
grow, go to the store and buy seeds. Read instructions on the
packets carefully and discuss them with your child.

ACTIVITY 2

Help your child turn over the soil in his garden plot. Some people have their soil rototilled each spring, but unless you're doing this for your own larger garden, you won't need to get so sophisticated. Remember, your child's garden plot is small: perhaps only one yard wide and one or two yards long. Make sure the soil is thoroughly mixed up and exposed to the sunlight for at least a day before you plant. Do you have any compost (old leaves, grass clippings, orange peels, egg shells, etc.) to add to the soil to enrich it?

ACTIVITY 3

Follow the instructions on the packets of your seeds. Help your child plant the seeds, alternating vegetables between rows. This will also help cut down on the types of pests that thrive in the garden. When the seeds are planted, water the garden.

ACTIVITY 4

Your child may want to put up a sign that says, "Johnnie's Garden" (or whatever name he wants to call it). He may also want to put a twig at the start of each row with the seed packet over the top of it. This will remind him which vegetables he planted in those rows.

ACTIVITY 5

(Optional) Does your child want to put a fence around his garden? If there are animals around that might feast on the vegetables when they grow bigger, you might want to consider this. Find materials you already have and build a simple barrier that will discourage small animals.

ACTIVITY 6

You and your child need to monitor the garden every day. If the temperature is really hot, you may need to water it daily. And weeds will begin to grow. Remove them by hand when they become noticeable.

ACTIVITY 7

Harvest time! When your child's vegetables are ripe, help him pick them. It's exciting to pull them from the ground. Once you've got as many as you want, take them into the kitchen and wash them. Include them in your family's salad that night or save some of them for your next Garden Fresh Soup. Be sure to make enthusiastic comments about your child's vegetables at dinner, such as:

- How tender they are

- How healthy they are

- How good they taste, and

- How pleased you are with your child's gardening ability.

ACTIVITY 8

Continue to assist your child harvest and use vegetables until the ground freezes.

44

PET PROTECTOR

Background

Every day some animals are subjected to cruel tests and inhumane conditions. Many experiments performed on them are unnecessary. Whenever possible, it's better to use other methods and computer tests instead of animal tests.

Talk to your child about the protection of animals. Perhaps you have a family pet that your child loves. Discuss the various ways that she helps take care of it, such as feeding, watering, walking, or petting it.

Now talk about other animals. Ask your child if she is aware of the following:

• When some fishermen catch tuna fish, they crush or drown dolphins. Dolphins are gentle and smart, and some are in the endangered species category. That means we need to protect them or they may cease to be part of our world.

• Ivory comes from the tusks of elephants. Unfortunately, people kill elephants just for their tusks so they can sell the ivory.

• Some calves are confined in tiny crates for life to be sold as veal. The crates are so small that the baby calves can't sit down or even turn around.

• Many cosmetics are tested on animals. For example, some companies squirt shampoos in the eyes of rabbits to see how badly the rabbit's eyes swell up.

• When people wear fur coats, it means that animals had to die. Very often these animals' legs were caught in steel traps and they froze to death.

To be earth friendly, we should do what we can to put an end to these practices. Ask your child if she would like to become a Pet Protector. To be one, she needs to be able to tell the difference between some earth friendly and unfriendly animal practices.

Tell her that you'll read some practices to her. She should smile after each one she thinks is friendly, and make an unhappy face after each one she thinks is unfriendly.

The Goal
To encourage your child to include protection of animals under her definition of earth friendly; and to be able to identify earth friendly and unfriendly practices with respect to animals.

Age Range
8 - 11 years

Materials Needed
None

[For your convenience, the practices are marked with an (F) for Friendly or a (U) for Unfriendly.]

• Setting fresh water on the porch for wild birds
  (F) Birds are often thirsty in the winter

• Eating a tuna fish sandwich
  (U) If dolphins were crushed in the process; but
  (F) If fishermen caught tuna without crushing dolphins

- Buying a beautiful ivory carving for Dad's birthday
  (U) Could mean an elephant was killed just for its tusks

- Taking your dog to the vet for his annual shots
  (F) Keeps your pet from getting diseases

- Buying a cruelty-free shampoo for the family
  (F) Means it wasn't tested on animals

- Ordering veal at a restaurant
  (U) The baby calf was probably caged in a tiny crate for its entire life

- Telling a clerk that you won't shop in her store because she sells fur coats
  (F) Fur means an animal was probably killed in a steel trap just for its fur

- Eating vegetarian meals several times a month
  (F) Saves animals' lives, and also helps stop the greenhouse effect

- Writing a letter to your Congressman asking him to pass a law that regulates animal testing
  (F) Will reduce cruelty to animals

- Changing your cat's kitty litter regularly
  (F) Gives your cat a fresh place to do its "business"

- Finding plastic rings from six-packs of pop lying on the beach and not picking them up
  (U) If they're not picked up, they could strangle seals or other creatures

- Making sure that your pet's water is fresh daily
  (F) Your pet counts on you for fresh water

Be sure to praise your child for being a "Pet Protector" whenever she uses earth friendly practices with regard to animals.

45

LET'S GET POLITICAL!

Background

Although we can become more earth friendly on a personal level, the best way to bring about national change is through the political process. That means we need to influence our elected representatives. The more frequently they hear from us about environmental concerns, the more likely they are to pass laws that are earth friendly. The representatives who won't protect the environment can be voted out of office. All it takes is enough of us acting on our consciences.

Discuss several environmental issues with your child. Identify one or two that he feels strongly about. Some possibilities include:

- CFCs are damaging our ozone layer and endangering the earth. CFCs should be phased out now!

- Experiments on animals are often unnecessary and cruel. They should be regulated more closely and fines should be levied against companies that violate the regulations.

- Polluted oceans are killing fish and making beaches unsafe places to swim. Disposal of waste in the oceans must be reduced and eventually stopped.

- Nuclear reactors can be dangerous. Some are breeder reactors that make plutonium, one of the most harmful substances known to man. Plutonium is used to make nuclear bombs, and it is not possible to safely dispose of it. If an accident occurs at a nuclear reactor, the environment could be polluted with radiation. Until we better understand nuclear energy and its waste products, we should be extremely careful about building nuclear reactors.

- The slaughter of dolphins and elephants is intolerable. Laws need to be passed immediately to protect these endangered species, and they should be strictly enforced.

- The sale of ivory from killing live animals should be stopped.

- Air pollution is responsible for lung cancer and other health problems. Demand that the companies responsible for polluting the air clean it up.

- Other

The Goal

To involve your child in the political process at several levels, including city, state, and national; to increase his awareness of elected representatives' stands on the environment; and to interest him in supporting key legislation.

Age Range

8 - 12 years

Materials Needed

Paper and pen or typewriter or computer, directory of your state's elected officials, envelopes, stamps.

❖

 **ACTIVITY 1**

After your child has identified one or two issues that bother him the most, help him write a letter to his local, state and national elected representatives. In it he should express his concern and ask what specific things each representative is doing to address it. Be sure your child includes his name, address, and telephone number in the letter. Ask for a timely response.

ACTIVITY 2

When your child receives his responses in the mail, help him understand them. Are some of the responses too vague? Do they skirt the issue and claim support without specifically stating how they are working to solve the problem? Or worse yet, do any officials refuse to acknowledge a problem? Keep track of who your child thinks is doing a good job on environmental issues, and who isn't. Make a note about when the representatives are up for re-election. Perhaps this could become an election issue.

You might wish to caution your child that as important as the environment is, there are other issues that also need to be considered. For example, you may feel that a politician's record is poor and even though he pays lip service to the environment, he wouldn't be a good choice. Be sure to explain this to your child if it's the case in your district.

Write follow-up letters if necessary. If you and your child think officials aren't representing you very well, let them know about it. Tell them you want support for certain laws, and if you don't get it, you'll let other voters know about it.

ACTIVITY 3

When election time rolls around, don't let your child forget how certain representatives responded to his concerns. Perhaps you and your child would like to make a donation to the campaign of someone who cares about the environment. Or there are lots of other ways for kids to get involved in campaigns. Some are:

- Filling helium balloons (but never for release into the atmosphere)

- Addressing envelopes

- Taping up posters around town

- Cleaning windows or doors at the campaign headquarters
- Helping set up tables and chairs at fund raising events
- Arranging food for snacks at "Meet the Candidate" functions
- Decorating the place where an event will be held
- Distributing brochures to people that explain the Candidate's positions
- Riding in a parade and wearing your Candidate's button
- Holding a sign on a street corner the day of the election

ACTIVITY 4

Sit down with your child just before election day and talk about who to vote for. Even if you haven't contributed time or money to any campaigns, you know how certain representatives responded to your child's earlier letters. Discuss why you think someone would do a good job and see what your child has to say.

ACTIVITY 5

On election day, take your child with you to the voting booth. You may not be able to let him come inside the booth itself, but he will see the process up close. When you come out, tell him what you did behind the curtain. Thank him for helping you make up your mind which representatives to vote for. Remind him that he's only got X number of years until he's 18 and can vote, too. Watch election returns on TV together or read about them in the paper the next day.

ACTIVITY 6

Monitor the performance of the representatives who were newly elected as well as those who were re-elected. Are they living up to their campaign promises to protect and maintain a healthy environment? If not, remind them about it. Continue to write letters and urge them to take action. Remember, time is running out!

46

INVISIBLE ENEMIES

Background

Gas stations with leaking underground storage tanks are a problem across the United States. In 1986 the Steel Tank Institute estimated that 350,000 tanks filled with gasoline would leak during the next five years. That's an average of 7,000 leaking tanks per state. Regulations were passed to reduce the amount of gasoline that leaks from these buried tanks into our ground water. New leakproof storage tanks are preventing additional gasoline leaks, but we're a long way from solving the problem with older tanks.

Explain the leaking tank problem to your child. Be sure to point out that leaking underground storage tanks are not limited to just gasoline from gas stations. They can also include home gas and oil tanks, septic tanks, and other chemical storage tanks.

Now ask your child if he'd like to see how buried tanks can secretly pollute the ground water. Collect the different materials and plan to put them together outside or in your garage.

The Goal

To demonstrate to your child how a leaking buried tank pollutes the ground water; and to increase his commitment to solving the problem through an awareness of the damage this causes.

Age Range

8 - 11 years

Materials Needed

Old aquarium, four cartons that held fresh strawberries (the plastic kind with open squares), moss, pebbles, dirt, a medium-size plastic bottle, pocket knife, water, red food coloring, and an old toy car, pencil and paper.

ACTIVITY 1

Help your child line the bottom of the aquarium with the upside-down strawberry cartons. Then add enough water so that it comes to the top of the cartons. Assist your child to place a two-inch thick layer of moss directly on top of the cartons. Then add a couple inches of dirt.

Next, fill the plastic bottle with water and several drops of red food coloring. You might wish to cut a small hole in the plastic bottle yourself, rather than letting your child do it—unless he's very careful. Now place the bottle horizontally in the dirt and bury it. Remember to place the bottle so that the hole is facing downward, so the fluid will drain into the dirt.

↑ upside-down strawberry containers ↑

Ask your child to set a toy car above the ground to indicate that it is a service station and that's where the car gets filled with gasoline.

Note what time it is. You may wish to write the day and time on a sheet of paper. What color is the water?

ACTIVITY 2

Periodically check the aquarium. When you think the water in the plastic bottle has drained into the dirt, pour a quart of tap water over the surface of the ground (to represent rainwater). How long does it take the ground water to turn red? Is the ground water slightly red or very red? If necessary, sprinkle more water over the surface of the ground.

Ask your child this question: If a person was unable to see what was happening below the ground, how would he know that the ground water was being polluted?

What would your child suggest as a solution to the older gas stations that have leaking underground tanks? Should they be shut down or allowed to continue operating? (This might make a great discussion as you both clean up.)

Hint: How about writing a letter to your Congressman or Congresswoman to see what's happening in your state? Perhaps some laws have been passed recently that deal with older gas tanks.

47

A SPECIAL EDITION OF "60 MINUTES"

Background

Environmental abuses are everywhere. Unfortunately, we don't have to look far to find out about oil spills, polluted air, leaking storage tanks, or mistreatment of animals. One of the most effective ways to do something about these abuses is to call them to the attention of the public. And what better way than through the media?

Explain to your child that investigative reporters look beyond the information that is "spoon-fed" to them. They double-check facts, talk to other sources, and get to the bottom of situations where they believe someone is trying to mislead the public. Investigative reporters don't accept simple answers to questions. They challenge the statements people make in an attempt to get to the truth. They know that by facing the truth, we can solve problems before they become worse.

Before you proceed with this activity, make sure your child understands that most gas stations and oil companies try very hard not to pollute the environment. They are concerned about the environment and go to great lengths to protect it. However, there are always a few companies that try to get away with environmental abuses. Those few are the ones that investigative reporters target, such as in this chapter.

Key Concepts

- Review the definition of **Leaking Underground Storage Tanks** (Chapter 46) with your child. Make sure he remembers how gasoline leaks into ground water and pollutes it.

- **Benzene** is a cancer-causing chemical that is found in oil and gasoline. It pollutes the earth and makes ground water unsafe to drink.

- An **oil tanker** is a large ship that carries oil from one destination to another.

- **Double-hulled bottoms** are the double steel bottoms on oil tankers. For many years environmentalists have been trying to convince oil companies and ship builders that it is safer to build double-hulled bottoms on oil tankers. It's not foolproof, but at least if a tanker crashes into a rock there is a double layer of protection.

Ask your child to be the Junior Reporter in the following two interviews, with you playing the part of the person being interviewed. Review the interviews with him before you start. That way he'll be familiar with the story lines and know what to expect. However, both of you should ad lib throughout and expand on details whenever you wish.

The Goal
To acquaint your child with the methods used by investigative reporters to expose environmental abuses; and through his participation in two interviews, to increase his understanding of why this is beneficial to society.

Age Range
8 - 12 years

Materials Needed
Table, chairs, medium-sized cardboard box (with a square base of 16-20 inches), scissors or pocket knife, puppet, kitchen timer, camcorder and VCR (optional).

Before You Start
Cut out the bottom of the cardboard box, leaving a border of about 1 inch. Set the box on its side at the edge of the table and arrange two chairs behind it. You and your child will sit on these chairs, and from the front it will appear as if you are on TV. If you have a camcorder and wish to tape these interviews, set up your camcorder on a tripod or have another member of the family videotape you.

If possible, use a puppet to represent yourself so that the space in the TV screen (the box) won't be so crowded.

When you're ready, set the kitchen timer so that it's ticking nearby as you talk. This adds the special flavor of an edition of "60 Minutes."

❖

INTERVIEW 1
The Leaking Tank Scandal

JR.: Good evening, Mr. Potts. Thank you for appearing on this Special Edition of 60 Minutes.

YOU: Good evening.

JR.: Mr. Potts, is it true that you own several gas stations in our town?

YOU: [Proudly] It certainly is! In fact, I'd say that I'm probably the biggest gas station owner in this part of the country.

JR.: So you make a good living operating your gas stations?

YOU: [Laughs] I would say that's a fair statement.

JR.: Mr. Potts, I understand that several people who live around your gas stations have recently found benzene in their water.

YOU: Yeah, that's what they're saying.

JR.: Do you think it's possible that your gas stations are responsible for this situation?

YOU:	Nope.
JR.:	Can you estimate how many underground storage tanks you have at each gas station?
YOU:	Oh, I don't know. Probably three or four.
JR.:	And how old are these tanks?
YOU:	How should I know? I wasn't around when they were buried.
JR.:	When did you buy your gas stations?
YOU:	Oh, 20—maybe 25—years ago.
JR.:	And were the gasoline tanks already buried when you bought the stations?
YOU:	Of course.
JR.:	So the buried gasoline tanks are 20-25 years old. Have you replaced any of them with newer tanks?
YOU:	No way. Newer tanks cost too much.
JR.:	So your older tanks could be leaking.
YOU:	I didn't say that!
JR.:	But Mr. Potts, your buried gasoline tanks are at least 20-25 years old. We all know that the older tanks weren't built as well as the new ones. And several of your neighbors have told me that their water has traces of benzene in it.
YOU:	SO??? They can't prove it was my fault!
JR.:	Actually, I think they can. All your neighbors have to do is complain to the Environmental Protection Agency, and EPA can shut down your business while they investigate.
YOU:	Well, what do those lousy neighbors want? If my business gets shut down, they won't have any gas to drive their cars with. That would serve them right!

JR.:	Perhaps you're not aware of this, Mr. Potts, but people everywhere have a right to drink clean water. And we won't put up with people who pollute it. There are plenty of gas stations around with good storage tanks.
YOU:	[Whining] But it would cost too much money to dig up my old tanks and put new ones in. I don't have enough money to do that.
JR.:	Excuse me, Mr. Potts, but didn't you brag about having the biggest gas stations in this part of the country? And didn't you also say that you make a pretty good living at it?
YOU:	Well, yes, but... [sputters off into silence]
JR.:	Thank you, Mr. Potts.

INTERVIEW 2
The Double-Hull Cop-Out

JR.:	Mr. Steel, is it true that you're the Chairman of one of the largest oil companies in the world?
YOU:	Yes, and I'm proud of it.
JR.:	How would you say your company is doing financially, Mr. Steel?
YOU:	Very well.
JR.:	I agree. I see from your last quarterly report that your company's profits are increasing. In fact, your company has made more money this past year than in any other year since you've been in business.
YOU:	[Smiling] That's right. We're doing great.
JR.:	Mr. Steel, I wonder if you'd like to comment on

the fact that your company has stopped using double-hulled oil tankers.

YOU: Sure. They cost too much. Tankers with only one bottom are cheaper, that's why we've switched to them.

JR.: But isn't it true that double-hulled tankers are safer than ones that have just one bottom?

YOU: It depends on what you mean by "safe."

JR.: By "safe" I mean that if one of your tankers has a double hull and it runs into a rock in the ocean, there's less chance that it will rip open and spill oil into the water.

YOU: Using that definition, I would agree that it's possible. I didn't say I agreed, mind you; I just said it might be possible.

JR.: If the oil companies were using double-hulled tankers, do you think the Exxon Valdez would have spilled oil off the coast of Alaska, in Prince William Sound?

YOU: I wouldn't want to venture an opinion on that.

JR.: Why not?

YOU: Because.

JR.: I see. Let me ask you another question, Mr. Steel. You say it costs too much to buy double-hulled tankers. But don't you think it costs a lot more to clean up oil spills? Oil spills that might not have happened in the first place if you'd bought double-hulled tankers?

YOU: I wouldn't want to venture an opinion on that.

JR.: I see. Thank you, Mr. Steel.

❖

After the Interviews: If you've videotaped the interviews, watch them with your child. Discuss some of the following questions:

- What does your child think of Mr. Potts' and Mr. Steel's claims that their companies can't afford better equipment because it's too expensive?

- Is this kind of attitude earth friendly?

- What would happen if investigative reporters didn't uncover abuses like this and call them to the public's attention? Would the companies be less likely to change their actions?

- What might happen as a result of the TV interviews? Would viewers be upset enough to pressure their representatives to pass stricter laws?

- What else might happen?

48

SECRET INDOOR ROBBERS

Background

Unfortunately, the air inside our homes can be more polluted than the outside air. This is because the air in our homes circulates less and contains many more pollutants than we realize.

Ask your child to pretend that she is Inspector Clue-so. Her mission is to dress as the Inspector and accompany you around the house to find the "Secret Indoor Robbers" that are polluting the air inside your home.

Review some known indoor robbers with your child:

• *Dirty air conditioners* contain germs that cause allergies. Pollutants breed in air ducts and drains that have not been cleaned regularly.

• *Carbon Monoxide* is caused by burning anything indoors. Some offenders are tobacco smoke, gas stoves, furnaces, a car running in the garage, and indoor grills. Old fashioned kerosene heaters and Franklin stoves release carbon monoxide into the air.

• *Radon* is an invisible, odorless and tasteless gas that poses a severe risk to your health. Radon is caused by the radioactive decay of uranium. If radon is found in the soil beneath your home, it could be drawn inside through air pressure. Children are particularly susceptible to the dangers of radon.

- *Asbestos* is a fibrous mineral that was widely used to make vinyl floor tiles, reinforced cement, fire-retardant materials, and pipe insulation. People exposed to asbestos dust suffer from lung disease and may eventually die of heart failure or cancer.

- *Mothball crystals and air fresheners* introduce dangerous chemicals to your home's air. Ironically, air fresheners claim to improve the quality of the air; in reality, they merely coat your nostrils with chemicals so that you don't smell the other odors.

- *Formaldehyde* is a preserving agent that causes cancer. It may be found in your furniture, carpet, particle boards, and foam insulation.

- *Dry cleaning fluid* used on clothes in your closet releases chemicals into the air.

- *Paint strippers and thinners* release methylene chloride into the air.

- Other

When your child is dressed as Inspector Clue-so and has her clipboard and pen in hand, she's ready to identify the "Secret Indoor Robbers" in your home. She may want to carry the magnifying glass and flashlight in her pockets.

The Goal

To help your child identify the secret indoor pollutants that rob your home of clean air, and to suggest ways to catch these robbers and get rid of them.

Age Range

7 - 11 years

Materials Needed

A trench coat, dark glasses, hat, magnifying glass (optional), flashlight, clipboard with paper and pen.

ACTIVITY 1

Accompany your child through each room in your home, including the garage and laundry room. Ask her to write down the names of each robber she can identify. Don't be afraid to examine dark, out-of-the-way places with the flashlight.

ACTIVITY 2

When you've made a thorough inspection of your home, sit down at the kitchen table and review the list. Which robbers can you do something about?

A few suggestions include:

- Be sure to regularly clean air ducts, drains or filters from your home's air conditioning system.

- Don't allow people to smoke indoors. But if you do, increase the air circulation, promptly dispose of ashes and keep ash trays clean.

- Never leave a car running in the garage.

- Have your furnace serviced annually.

- Buy a radon-testing kit at your local hardware store. They are inexpensive and easy to use. If your home has a problem with radon, find out how to ventilate it properly. Your radon testing kit should include further information about sources of assistance, or call your nearest Cooperative Extension service.

- Asbestos may not be as easy to get rid of. If your home is 20-

50 years old and you suspect you have a problem with asbestos, call one or more general contractors and see what they recommend.

- Stop using mothballs and air fresheners. Try to eliminate the source of odors.

- If you're buying new furniture or carpet, check the labels. Avoid materials that have been treated with formaldehyde.

- Buy clothes that don't need to be dry cleaned. Reduce the frequency of cleaning of clothes you already own that need to be dry cleaned.

- Tightly close lids on paint and paint thinners so that chemicals are not released into the air.

- Dispose of materials properly if they are considered hazardous waste (see Chapter 10).

ACTIVITY 3

Take action against any robbers that you and your Inspector think are threatening your home's indoor air. This may be as simple as cleaning ash trays or it may be more time-consuming, such as buying a radon-testing kit. Whatever form of action you and your child decide to take, make sure she feels good about it. After all, these robbers are secretly hurting her—and she's discovering them and getting rid of them.

49

DESIGNER HOMES

Background

Although many of our present homes have features that are unfriendly to the earth, that doesn't mean the homes of the future have to. By knowing what to include and what to avoid, we can encourage architects to design earth friendly homes for our children.

Review with your child the following features of a home that are earth friendly:

- Solar panels are a way of capturing the sun's energy and using it to heat homes. This lessens the need for such nonrenewable fossil fuels as coal, oil or natural gas. If the home will be built in a warm climate, can solar energy be substituted for all or some of the heating system?

- Square homes use energy more efficiently than other shapes.

- Good ventilation systems eliminate the danger of radon gas being trapped in the home. With positive pressure inside the home, it is also possible to prevent radon from entering.

- Well insulated walls don't waste energy. However, be sure there is good air exchange in the home because super-insulated homes can trap air pollutants inside.

- Carpets are available that haven't been treated with formaldehyde.

- Showers can be installed with low-flow shower heads, and toilets are available that don't waste unnecessary water.

- Water heaters with an "energy conservation" setting don't use as much energy to heat water.

- Latex paint is more earth friendly than oil-based paint.

- A recycling center close to the kitchen could include separate bins for glass, aluminum, tin, paper and plastic items.

- Using pine or birch saves tropical hardwoods, which means that more rainforests will be saved.

- Trees around the house are not only attractive, they are earth friendly.

- A graywater tank under the house can collect water from the shower and sink. This is used to sprinkle the garden and lawn instead of ground water from a well.

- Other

Ask your child to pretend that she is a famous designer who has been selected to design an earth friendly home. She should take into account the features she just reviewed when designing this home.

The Goal
To encourage your child to design an earth friendly home, and to be able to identify its earth friendly features.

Age Range
5 - 10 years

Materials Needed
Crayons or colored pencils, paper.

ACTIVITY 1

Ask your child to design an earth friendly home. She may wish to draw an outside view as well as an inside view. Whenever she includes an earth friendly feature, ask her to label it. She may not know how to spell some of the words, so be prepared to help her. Encourage her to use her imagination.

ACTIVITY 2

When she is finished, admire the design. Let her point out how the different earth friendly features operate. Tape it to a wall in your home so that other members of the family can admire it too. Later when you take it down, your child might wish to keep it in a scrap book.

50

DESIGNER CITIES

Background

The way our cities are laid out often reflect an insensitivity to the earth. Developers disregard forests, open fields, and other natural areas. In addition, some of the zoning laws do not make sense from an environmental point of view. As we become more earth friendly, our architects and planners will place more emphasis on environmental factors when they design new projects.

Make sure your child knows that a *zoning law* is a law that tells you what kind of buildings can be built on a piece of property. For example, a zoning law might say that all property within a certain area has to have single family homes. We call that a *residential* zone. Another zoning law might say that only businesses can be located in an area. We call that a *commercial* zone.

Review the following earth friendly features with your child before he begins designing the city:

• Open fields should be protected wherever possible.

• Forests should also be protected as much as possible.

• Streams and ponds should be left in their natural state. Rather than filling them in, development could take place around them.

- Zoning laws could be changed so that houses could be grouped closer together in exchange for large open areas that surround the houses. Everyone would be able to use and enjoy the open areas.

- Shopping malls and commercial space could be built within walking distance of the houses. This would reduce the need for transportation.

- One or more parks could be added to the town to enhance its attractiveness.

- Zoning laws could be changed so that certain areas are not only for commercial or residential use. That way clusters of homes, workplaces, stores, and cultural centers could all be grouped together.

- Find out everything possible about the natural climate of the land before designing a city. If an area floods regularly, don't build there. Save money on landscaping, insurance and damage control by investigating the conditions of the area first.

- Look at the way older rural cities are built to see if there are other ways to design cities in harmony with the earth.

- Ensure that individual homes in the city also have earth friendly features.

- Minimize the areas with pavement. This allows more rainwater to enter the ground and replenish the ground water.

- Other

Ask your child to pretend that he is a famous designer who has been selected to design an earth friendly city. He should take into account the features he just reviewed before designing the city.

The Goal

To encourage your child to design an earth friendly city, and to be able to identify those features that make it earth friendly.

Age Range

   5 - 10 years

Materials Needed

   Crayons or colored pencils, paper.

ACTIVITY 1

Ask your child to design an earth friendly city. Whenever he includes an earth friendly feature, ask him to label it. Be prepared to help him with the spellings, and again, encourage him to be imaginative.

ACTIVITY 2

Admire the design and post it next to your child's drawing of an earth friendly home. Later you might wish to take it down and include it in a scrap book.

51

RECIPE FOR A FRIENDLY EARTH

Background

Explain to your child that you would like him to create an
imaginary recipe. In other words, it's not something that can
be cooked in the kitchen; it's a list of ingredients that will
make the earth a more friendly place, written in recipe format.
The cookbook is merely a resource to trigger ideas for meas-
urements and directions. After you and your child read the
following two recipes, ask him to create his own.

The Goal

To write an imaginary recipe for a friendly earth, using
ingredients that are based on your child's knowledge of the
environment.

Age Range

7 - 11 years

Materials Needed

Cookbook, paper and pen.

RECIPE 1

1/2 C fresh water
1 lb caring concern for the earth
1 dash attention, sprinkled with urgency
1/2 T morning sunlight, filtered
2 lb leaves from undisturbed rainforest trees
1 C fresh vegetables, organically grown

Mix all ingredients in large bowl. Add 2 parts love to 1 part
commitment and thoroughly stir together. Bake at 250 until
done. Garnish with tenderness. Serves family of four.

RECIPE 2

2 T recyclable products, separated
1/2 C clean air
1 lb fruit, organically grown
2/3 C bird seed for bird feeders
1 dash fresh cloth, lightly scented
6 paper shopping bags, well used

Mix recyclable products and seeds together, stirring gently.
Add other items one at a time. Sprinkle a dash of flowers over
the mixture in an artistic arrangement. Cook at 375 for 30
minutes, or until firm in the center. Serves family of four.

Now it's time for your child to try his own imaginary recipes!

52

EARTH RESOLUTIONS

Background

Now that your child has a good idea of what it takes to be earth friendly, she needs to translate this into action for the coming year. What better way than through Earth Resolutions, similar to New Year's Resolutions? All it takes is a willingness to set small goals and stick to them.

Ask your child if she knows what New Year's Resolutions are. She has probably heard adults make promises at the end of December about what they plan to do in the next year. If so, she knows that these are good intentions and that people will try to live up to them. Earth Resolutions are your child's promises to be more earth friendly in the coming year.

There are many different Earth Resolutions that your child might identify. Some ideas are:

- To stop wasting water when I take a shower

- To recycle aluminum cans, glass, and newspapers

- To volunteer one hour a month at an earth friendly place

- To turn off the lights whenever I leave my room
- To remind Mom and Dad to take paper bags to the store
- To refuse to accept food in styrofoam containers
- To plant a garden
- To take better care of my toys
- To donate toys I don't use anymore to a charity instead of throwing them out
- To write two letters to my Congressman about issues that affect the earth
- To groom my dog regularly
- To eat three vegetarian meals a month
- Other

The Goal

To help your child set five (5) Earth Resolutions for the coming year, and to help her abide by them.

Age Range

4 - 12 years

Materials Needed

Paper and pen.

These are just examples. Your child may have different ideas about what she wants to identify as her Earth Resolutions.

ACTIVITY 1

Assist your child to think of her own Earth Resolutions. She should write them on a piece of paper and number them from 1 to 5.

ACTIVITY 2

Post your child's Earth Resolutions in a place where she will see them often. If you notice her neglecting one or more of the Resolutions during the year, remind her of them. With both of you keeping track, it will be much easier to maintain your child's earth friendly attitude.

Questions
and
Answers

QUESTIONS & ANSWERS

1. *What is ACID RAIN?*

Acid rain is polluted rainwater. It is caused by burning fossil fuels such as coal and oil. When these fuels are burned they release sulfur and nitrogen into the air. If moisture is present in the air, sulfuric and nitric acids are formed. These acid particles return to earth with rain.

Sometimes this process is called "acid precipitation" or "acid deposition" because solid particles can also be polluted when they return to the earth. In other words, snow and hail can be acid as well as rain.

Any form of acid precipitation is harmful to fish. In parts of Canada fish have disappeared from hundreds of lakes. On the east coast of the United States, acid precipitation has had a severe impact on lakes. If it is not brought under control, the fish and plants and other microorganisms in our lakes could disappear in the next 10 to 20 years.

Acid rain is also harmful to trees, forests and other living things. It is a worldwide problem that needs to be addressed quickly.

2. *How can I tell if the AIR I breathe is polluted?*

Most air pollution in the United States is caused by motor vehicles and industry. In cities with a lot of industrial plants, air pollution shows up as a gray haze, especially on wet winter mornings. Most of this is from the burning of coal. In cities where motor vehicles are numerous, air pollution shows up as a yellow smog. This is sometimes referred to as "photochemical smog."

Such smog may be dense enough to irritate people's eyes and lungs. Additionally, air pollution can cause cancer and respiratory illnesses. Smog is infamous in Los Angeles, California, but now it is also found in most major cities of the United States. Pollutants in the atmosphere can also return to the earth as acid rain.

It's not always possible to tell if the air you breathe is polluted, but the presence of haze or smog is a strong indicator.

3. What's the matter with ANIMAL TESTING?

Animals have been used in many inhumane tests that are not essential to human survival or comfort. For example, we don't need to kill or maim animals just to find out whether a new eye shadow, lipstick or shampoo is safe. Many of these experiments could be done with computer models or other methods.

Some medical tests may be necessary to find cures for diseases. When there is no other way to test life-saving cures, animal tests should be conducted in as painless and humane a way as possible. Animals are an important part of our environment. We should never forget that they experience pain, loneliness and fear—just as humans do.

4. Why is ASBESTOS a problem?

Asbestos contains fibers that have strength and resistance to heat. That's why asbestos was used to make clothes for protecting fire fighters and reinforcing concrete. It was also used in the insulation for buildings, and it is still used in automobile brake linings.

However, asbestos dust is dangerous. When people breathe it, it can scar their lungs. Victims who have been exposed to asbestos dust can have trouble breathing, and the exposure may result in lung cancer or heart failure.

5. **What happens when I release a helium BALLOON into the air?**

The balloon floats up into the air. As it rises, it expands due to the sun's heat and the reduced pressure in the atmosphere. Then it pops and falls back to earth. It might land in the woods, or your backyard, or the ocean. Animals can come across them and eat them. Fish who swallow balloons can die. That's why releasing balloons into the air is not an earth friendly thing to do.

6. **What is BENZENE?**

Benzene is a colorless liquid that comes chiefly from coal tar. It is found in oil and gas, and it is used to make plastics. When underground storage tanks leak, benzene may permeate down through the soil into the ground water and contaminate it. Benzene is dangerous to your health because it is a chemical known to cause cancer.

7. **What does BIODEGRADABLE mean?**

A biodegradable material is something that can be broken down or decomposed. Usually bacteria (very small plants) break down materials. Some materials decompose faster than other materials. Once they are decomposed, biodegradable materials can be returned to the soil and re-used in a cycle of earth friendly materials.

8. **Why should I try BORIC ACID to get rid of indoor pests?**

Boric acid has a less noticeable smell than many other chemicals. That means insects can't detect and avoid it as easily as other pesticides. In one study, boric acid was more effective in the fight against cockroaches than several other chemicals. After 10 years of use, cockroaches have still not developed a resistance to boric acid.

But even boric acid can have negative impacts. After all, it is an acid. If you use it, use it cautiously and conservatively.

9. What is a CARCINOGEN?

A carcinogen is a substance that tends to cause cancer. Cancer is a tumor that makes cells grow and divide abnormally fast. Some tumors grow so fast they can't be controlled, and they kill nearby tissues. Eventually this kind of cancer results in death.

10. What are CFCs?

CFC is the abbreviation for Chlorofluorocarbon. CFCs are gases used to make aerosol sprays, refrigerators, styrofoam and air conditioners. When CFCs are released into the air, they are not readily broken down. They rise to the highest levels of the atmosphere until the sun's intense light breaks them down. As this happens, CFCs release chlorine atoms that break down the ozone layer. The ozone layer is important because it protects us from ultraviolet rays, which can cause skin cancer.

11. Is there any safe way to dispose of CFCs?

Once CFCs have been produced, the best way to dispose of them is through recycling. Certified officials can recycle the CFCs in a refrigerator to other refrigerators, for example. Other than recycling, there is no fool-proof way to dispose of CFCs without damaging the ozone layer. The proposed strategy is to eliminate the use of CFCs worldwide and substitute more earth friendly products.

12. What is COMPOSTING?

Composting is placing yard, garden and kitchen waste into a pile and letting microorganisms turn it into compost. Compost is partially decomposed vegetation. It makes an excellent soil conditioner for lawns and gardens. People who understand the environment value compost, because it helps create beautiful, natural, earth friendly yards.

13. What does CONSERVATION mean?

Conservation is the careful use of resources, so that people benefit both now and in the future. People who care about conservation realize that some resources can be used up too quickly or completely. That's why they use resources wisely.

People who practice conservation methods will recycle products, reduce their use of some products, and choose materials that are not harmful to the environment.

14. What is DEFORESTATION?

Deforestation means cutting down or burning trees in an area and not replanting them. Deforestation is harmful because it reduces the number of trees that produce oxygen for us to breathe. Some trees may contain the cures for medical diseases. If we cut them down, they won't be available to help us in the future. Deforestation can also hurt the earth, because bare land may be washed away (or eroded) by rain. This results in a loss of nutrients to the soil. In addition, trees help slow down the greenhouse effect because they use carbon dioxide. Without them, global warming could speed up.

15. Can the earth friendly things I do really make a DIFFERENCE?

Yes! It all starts with one person—you. By taking little steps, you help save trees, water, air, and landfill space. You influence others around you, such as your family and friends. And sooner than you realize, your little steps multiply to big results.

Every earth friendly practice you adopt makes a big difference!

16. What's the matter with DISPOSABLE products?

Disposable products are wasteful. They're meant for one-time use and then they end up at the landfill or sewage treatment plant. With landfill space shrinking so quickly, disposable items are not a wise choice.

17. What does ECOLOGY mean?

Ecology is the study of how living things relate to each other and to their environment.

18. What is an ECOSYSTEM?

An ecosystem is all of the living things present in a certain area, along with their physical environment. Some ecosystems have more diversity (or number of different species) than others.

In an ecosystem, the size of a natural population is based on how many resources there are in the area, how much competition there is, and how many predators there are. In general, species diversity is an indicator of a healthy system. The reverse is also true—species extinction is an indicator of an unhealthy system.

19. What is an ENDANGERED SPECIES?

A species is a group of animals or plants with characteristics in common. It becomes endangered when conditions threaten its existence. There are about 5 million species on earth, but biologists expect that fully 1 million species will disappear by the year 2000 because people are destroying their habitat, or living place.

The fate of a species in the 20th century often depends on how compatible it is with human populations. If a species has few individuals, there is a greater chance that it will die out. Or if a species needs large areas, is not competitive with other species, or is hunted by people, it may not be able to survive.

The bald eagle is one example of an endangered species. Once a species is recognized as an endangered species, the law protects it.

20. What does the ENVIRONMENTAL PROTECTION AGENCY do?

The United States Environmental Protection Agency (USEPA) is a department of the federal government. It is responsible for enforcing environmental laws and regulating pollution of the air, land and water. The EPA is the "policeman" for the environment.

21. What is GLOBAL WARMING?

Global warming is the increasing temperature of the earth. It is caused by gases (mainly carbon dioxide and methane) that produce the greenhouse effect.

22. What is the GREENHOUSE EFFECT?

The greenhouse effect is the heating of the earth. It is caused by gases in the air that trap heat and keep it from escaping into space. Like a greenhouse, the earth lets in sunlight and keeps heat from escaping.

The greenhouse effect is caused mostly by carbon dioxide (from burning fossil fuels), methane (from cattle and landfills), and nitrous oxides (from burning wood and fossil fuels).

The danger is that by increasing the earth's temperature too much, we will alter our climate. This could melt ice caps in the Arctic and Antarctic, which would raise the sea level and sink cities on the coast. Also, it could change our weather patterns and turn our farmlands into deserts.

Some scientists are not convinced that we are causing global warming. Rather, they think that we are just experiencing fluctuating weather patterns. Some "models" even suggest that we are experiencing global cooling.

Unfortunately, Earth did not come with a book of instructions. When we attempt to predict the future, we are sometimes wrong. However, we try to analyze trends so that we can take corrective action before some of them become irreversible.

23. What is GROUND WATER?

Ground water is the water that is under the surface of the earth. About one third of the water that falls on earth filters down through the soil and forms ground water. This water accumulates in air pockets between soil particles, and usually has sand or gravel in it.

24. What is GROUND WATER CONTAMINATION?

Ground water contamination is when a supply of ground water is polluted, or contaminated. This could happen by spilling oil, gas, pesticides, chemicals or sewage onto the surface of the ground. Such pollutants filter down through the soil until they reach ground water. It doesn't take much to contaminate the water for entire areas. Once ground water is contaminated, it is very difficult to clean up.

25. What is GROUND WATER DEPLETION?

Ground water depletion is when the supply of ground water is used up, or depleted. Since the water cycle may take hundreds of years to replace ground water, our supply can be used faster than it is replaced.

26. What is a HABITAT?

A habitat is the physical area where an organism lives. Two things control the kind of plants that live in a habitat: temperature and rainfall. In places that receive a lot of rain, you can expect to find large trees. And places with lighter rainfall may only have small trees or shrubs. Since plants are the source of food for many animals, the plants in a habitat also determine the other kind of organisms that can live there.

27. What is HAZARDOUS WASTE?

Hazardous waste is material that is harmful to the environment after we're done using it. Most waste used to be biodegradable. For example, common waste materials used to include manure, paper, wood, and leather. These materials can be broken down by organisms and recycled through the ecosystem.

But today's hazardous waste is a different story. There are about 35,000 artificial chemicals made in the United States. We know little about their long-term effects on the environment. Some hazardous waste materials never decompose, and some are very dangerous while they are decomposing.

Materials are generally considered to be hazardous when they pose a hazard to the health of plants, animals or humans, or when they present an immediate danger.

Common hazardous wastes include paint, paint thinner, oven and toilet cleaners, furniture strippers, car batteries, antifreeze and mothballs.

28. Why can't we burn trash in an INCINERATOR instead of taking it to the landfill?

Incineration, or burning of trash in a special furnace with pollution controls, is one way to reduce the volume of waste. But even our most modern incinerators can cause air pollution. They add gases, ash and other matter to the air. Waste may not burn completely even at very high temperatures, and the residue must still be disposed of at landfills.

Incineration is favored in some places such as Japan, which has little land available for landfills. It is also an alternative for large cities like Los Angeles and New York. However, incineration should not be a viable alternative unless energy recovery is practiced and recycling of nonrenewable resources is part of the process.

Incinceration burns organic materials, which took millions of years to produce, and converts them to carbon dioxide and other gases. Air pollution controls for an incinerator are complex and very costly. In addition, incineration could become a major contributor to the greenhouse effect. Generally speaking, incineration is only a short range solution to a long range problem.

29. What is a LANDFILL?

A landfill is an area that is used for dumping solid waste such as cardboard, paper, cans, glass, containers, and other materials. Most nonhazardous waste is deposited in landfills.

Every year Americans generate more than 4 billion tons of waste. This is about 100 pounds of waste per person per day, including mining wastes, agricultural residue, sewage sludge, industrial waste, and municipal refuse. (Municipal refuse is the solid waste collected by a city's garbage system and disposed of at the landfill.) Each of us produces about 8 pounds of municipal solid waste per person per day—or over a ton a year.

Landfills used to be open dumps where waste was sometimes burned and then left unmanaged. In 1976 Congress passed a law to stop open and burning dumps. It required existing dumps to be converted to sanitary landfills.

Sanitary landfills may be lined with clay to stop liquid wastes from getting into the ground water. Sanitary landfills may also need a treatment plant to clean up water that passes through the landfill. And in some places, methane gas from decomposing materials may need to be vented (or possibly recovered and used for energy) so that fires or explosions don't occur.

Landfills are known by the saying, "out of sight, out of mind." They are a short range solution to a long range process and they won't be acceptable in the future. Already we are running out of space for them, and public resistance to new landfills is growing. Often a reaction occurs that is called the NIMBY effect—Not In My Back Yard.

We will probably always need landfills for materials when there is no other way to dispose of them, but our indiscriminate dumping of materials in landfills should stop. About half of the materials that we currently throw out could be recycled. This would save both our natural resources and space at landfills.

30. *What are NATURAL RESOURCES?*
Natural resources are anything produced naturally that are used by a group of people. Fresh water, oil, trees, gold, and coal are some examples.

Some resources are renewable and others other nonrenewable. For an explanation of the difference, see the question about Renewable Resources.

31. *What is a NUCLEAR REACTOR?*
A nuclear reactor is a process that splits atoms to produce energy. The splitting of these atoms is done with a small amount of fuel—either uranium or plutonium. The energy (heat) produced by a nuclear reactor can be used for electricity.

Nuclear reactors do not burn fossil fuels, so in that sense they are easier on the environment. However, the radioactive waste that is left over from nuclear reactors is highly toxic and cannot be easily disposed of. It is a national and worldwide problem that so far has not been solved satisfactorily.

32. *What are NUTRIENTS?*
Nutrients are the organic matter added to soil. These are usually nitrogen, phosphorus, and trace minerals. The most fertile soil has dead plants and animals, animal urine and feces, and other microorganisms in it. These nutrients help retain water and protect the soil from the sun's heat. They also stimulate plant growth.

33. *What is the OZONE LAYER?*
The ozone layer is formed from oxygen and energy from the

sun. It is a protective barrier in the atmosphere, about 6 to 30 miles up. It surrounds the earth and screens out most of the sun's harmful ultraviolet rays.

34. What do we mean by OZONE DEPLETION?

Ozone depletion is what happens when the ozone layer is broken down, or depleted. We rely on the ozone layer to protect us from some of the sun's harmful rays. When this layer is depleted, more harmful rays reach the earth. CFCs are the main culprit in ozone depletion.

The ozone depletion over Antarctica is of great concern. This hole in the ozone layer is growing larger and could threaten life on earth.

35. What is OVERPOPULATION?

The human population, or number of people on earth, has grown faster during the 20th century than it ever has before. Today there are more than three times as many people as there were in 1900. Some reasons for this are that we have learned how to cure certain diseases and live in ways that increase our life expectancy.

The population of the world is nearing 6 billion and could double in 30 years. The population of the United States is currently about 250 million. With its present rate of growth, the United States population could reach 500 million by the year 2100.

One of the problems with overpopulation (having too many people on earth) is that there is more competition for natural resources. More forests are cut down, more water is used, more pollution is generated, more land is used, and more food is needed.

In countries where the population has stayed about the same, the quality of life is better. In areas with high birth rates, conditions remain poor or are getting worse.

36. How can I tell if a product has too much PACKAGING?

A few simple guidelines should help. First, look for vegetables that are loose, that is, not bagged in plastic. Try to buy products in larger quantities. Whenever possible, avoid products that include individually wrapped portions. For example, cheese with individually wrapped slices has too much packaging. Breakfast cereals with individually wrapped portions have too much packaging. And remember, it may be better to buy products with paper instead of plastic packaging—but be sure to consider all the impacts and alternatives.

37. What are PESTICIDES?

In general, pesticides are chemicals that people use to kill pests. Pests are often insects that people consider a nuisance. These pests may eat crops or get into homes and pester us in one way or another.

Pesticides have major drawbacks. For one thing, some pests have developed a resistance to them. That means stronger doses or different chemicals have to be used. In addition, pesticides can endanger the health of people, plants and animals. Once pesticides are used, they can get into our food supply, water supply, and soil. No one knows how much damage they may ultimately cause to the environment.

Present trends suggest the use of IPM, or Integrated Pest Management. IPM uses all options available to control pests and minimizes the use of chemicals.

38. What are PHOSPHATES?

Phosphates are chemicals that cause plants in water to grow very fast. These plants continue to grow until they have used up all the phosphates in the water, and then they die. When the plants decompose they use oxygen. This lack of oxygen hurts fish and other living things in the water, and it may cause them to die as well. (Eutrophication is the name given to this process of fertilizing the water system.)

39. Are PLASTIC products harder on the environment than paper products?

This is not an easy question to answer. At best, we can say, "Maybe."

In general, most plastic is resistant to biodegradation, although new types are being developed. Many plastic items are meant for one-time use, and they are extremely wasteful. Once deposited in landfills, plastic items may be there almost forever. Burning of plastics can release dangerous chemicals into the air. However, plastics also have advantages such as convenience and durability.

Paper products are developed from trees, which are a renewable resource. If the resource is used wisely, paper is a good product. But if use of paper means depletion of the rainforests, they aren't a wise choice. Some paper processes release harmful chemicals into the air. Also, burning of paper can cause air pollution and create carbon dioxide, a greenhouse gas. One-time use of paper may be as bad as one-time use of plastic. Paper does not degrade easily in landfills, but it will probably degrade faster than most plastics.

So, is use of paper products better than plastic? Maybe, but not necessarily. If the choice is whether to buy a one-time plastic or a one-time paper product at a grocery store, neither is a good choice. The best solution is to use returnable bags and returnable products.

40. What is PLUTONIUM?

Plutonium is a man-made byproduct of uranium. It is used to provide energy in nuclear reactors. Unfortunately, this plutonium-239 is also used to make nuclear bombs.

Plutonium is extremely dangerous because it is radioactive, or poisonous to living things. Further, plutonium stays radioactive for at least 24,000 years. This makes it a long-term problem for the environment.

Plutonium can cause radiation sickness, a higher rate of cancer, and death. Disposal of plutonium in buried tanks in the earth or ocean are not good solutions. Earthquakes could rupture these tanks and release plutonium into the air or sea at some time in the future. That's why people who care about the earth are so concerned about plutonium and the misuse of nuclear energy.

41. What is POLLUTION?

Pollution is anything that causes a degree of contamination in the air, water or soil which will harm living things. For example, air pollution may be caused by too many motor vehicles spewing carbon monoxide into the air. Water may become polluted when too many wastes are discharged into it. And soil may be polluted when pesticides are sprayed onto it. All forms of pollution can have a harmful effect on living things.

42. What does RADIATION mean?

Radiation refers to the invisible rays given off by a substance. Some rays are more harmful than others. For example, the radiation from an atomic bomb is very dangerous to living things. We also know that in high doses, radiation from x-rays can be carcinogenic. That's why we try to limit our exposure to them.

43. What is RADON?

Although you can't see, smell or taste radon, it can pose a risk to your health. It is a product from the decay of uranium, and it can be drawn into your home through air pressure. Children are particularly susceptible to the dangers of radon. This gas can result in lung cancer faster than if you were a chain smoker. It's a good idea to buy a radon test kit and test your home.

44. Why are RAINFORESTS so important?

Rainforests are some of the earth's richest ecosystems. Although they account for less than 10% of our land, they contain almost half of all animal and plant species. Unfortunately, more than half of the earth's rainforests have been cut down since 1945, and they are presently being reduced at the rate of 50,000 acres per day.

Hardwoods such as teak and mahogany come from rainforests. Some poverty-stricken countries need cash, so they cut down their rainforest trees to sell, or they use the land to raise cattle or crops. Once there are no trees to absorb rainfall, floods can occur. And the thin soil left behind soon loses its fertility and is subject to erosion.

Many of the species that lived within the rainforest die. Once these species are gone, they are gone forever. We can't replace them.

Rainforests are important because of the great variety of organisms that thrive there. Many plants and trees contain secrets that could be discovered and become cures for diseases. We need to protect these important ecosystems.

45. Why should I RECYCLE products?

Because you save the earth's nonrenewable resources. For example, there is only a limited amount of aluminum in the earth. Recycling aluminum cans means aluminum will be available indefinitely, and the earth won't run out of it.

Recycling also saves space at your landfill. With so many landfills filling up and new ones becoming harder to locate, it's important that you recycle every product possible. This means there will be less cost to develop new resources, less cost to dispose of waste, and less pollution to deal with. That equates to a healthier environment for all of us.

46. What's the difference between RENEWABLE and NONRENEWABLE RESOURCES?

Renewable resources are natural resources that can last indefinitely because they are produced continuously. For example, when a renewable resource dies, it produces off-spring that will replace it. Trees, corn, shrubs, animals, fish, and people are examples.

Nonrenewable resources are natural resources that can be used up completely. There is only a limited supply in the earth, and when they're gone, that's it. Some examples of nonrenewable resources are oil, coal, sand, aluminum, gold, and natural gas.

47. What's the long range solution to SOLID WASTE DISPOSAL?

The solution will involve an integrated system, including the prevention of waste, use of earth friendly products, use of returnable containers (such as glass, metal, and plastic), recycling, no burning except for energy recovery, biodegrada-tion of organic waste, severe penalties for waste and pollution, and an attitude of "what we do today we must live with tomorrow."

48. What's wrong with using STYROFOAM products?

Styrofoam is made with CFCs, which are harmful to the ozone layer. Many styrofoam containers are made for one-time use, so they are very wasteful and quickly end up in landfills. And once they're in landfills, they may not decompose for up to 500 years. That's why styrofoam is both harmful and wasteful.

49. What are TOXIC CHEMICALS?

Toxic chemicals are chemicals that are poisonous to living things such as people, plants and animals. Toxic chemicals include some pesticides, mercury, lead and other heavy metals, some waste of petrochemical products, and radioactive waste such as plutonium.

50. Why are TREES so important to us?

Trees release oxygen into the air for us to breathe. We exhale carbon dioxide, and this is used by trees in their growth process. Because trees use carbon dioxide, they also help control the greenhouse effect. Without them, life on earth would not be suitable for people. They also are a renewable resource if used properly, and we use wood products for many things.

51. What are ULTRAVIOLET RAYS?

Ultraviolet rays are energy from the sun. They are part of the sun's heat energy that can damage genetic material. They can cause skin cancer in people and kill other organisms. The ozone layer screens out most ultraviolet rays, but if the ozone continues to be depleted they will become a bigger problem.

52. What is the WATER CYCLE?

Water continuously travels through a cycle, known as the hydrologic or water cycle. As it evaporates from the earth, it forms water vapor. The vapor rises until it reaches cold air, condenses, and turns into clouds. Then it rains, and the cycle begins again. This water cycle is driven by the sun's heat energy, and it causes the water in every body of water to be replaced.

Resources
and
Index

RESOURCES

Arms, Karen. Environmental Science. Saunders College Publishing, Orlando, Florida, 1990.

Council on Economic Priorities. Shopping for a Better World: A Quick and Easy Guide to Socially Responsible Supermarket Shopping. Ballantine Books, New York, New York, 1989.

The Earthworks Group. 50 Simple Things You Can Do to Save the Earth. Earthworks Press, Berkeley, California, 1989.

The Earthworks Group. 50 Simple Things Kids Can Do to Save the Earth. Earthworks Press, Berkeley, California, 1990.

The Environmental Magazine. Developing a Development Ethic: Working with the Currents of Nature. Earth Action Network, Inc., Volume 1, Number 3, May/June 1990, pp. 25-27.

Heloise. Hints for a Healthy Planet. The Putnam Publishing Company, New York, New York, 1990.

Hoyt, John A. Personal Action Guide: A Project for The United Nations Environment Programme. The Humane Society of the United States, Washington, D.C., 1990.

Hoyt, John A. 101 Ways to Help Heal the Earth: A Citizens Guide. The Greenhouse Crisis Foundation, Washington, D.C., 1990.

Kourik, Robert. Combating Household Pests Without Chemical Warfare. Garbage, the Practical Journal for the Environment, Volume II, No. 2, March/April 1990, pp. 22-29.

MacEachern, Diane. Save our Planet: 750 Everyday Ways You Can Help Clean Up the Earth. Dell Publishing, New York, New York, 1990.

Purdom, P. Walton and Anderson, Stanley H. Environmental Science: Managing the Environment. Charles E. Merrill Publishing Company, Columbus, Ohio, 1983.

Waxman, Don. Teaching Restoration to Kids. Whole Earth Review, No. 66, Spring 1990, pp. 64-66.

INDEX

THIS IS TO CERTIFY THAT

_____
name

has completed the activities in

RAISING AN EARTH FRIENDLY CHILD, LEVEL I

and
is hereby declared to be

EARTH FRIENDLY

_____
Parent's signature and date

ABOUT THE AUTHOR

Debbie Tilsworth is executive director of a non-profit organization in Fairbanks, Alaska, a post she has held since 1987. She has a B.ed from the University of Alaska Fairbanks in Elementary Education (1982), and has substitute taught grades K-6. She has been employed by several organizations since 1972, including an environmental engineering firm. She has served on numerous Boards of Directors and been a volunteer for fund raising, political and human service organizations. She is married to Dr. Timothy Tilsworth, a Professor of Civil and Environmental Engineering at the University of Alaska Fairbanks. She and Tim own a Shetland Sheepdog business and breed, raise and show their dogs. Debbie has two stepsons, Craig and Pat.

Please share *your* earth friendly ideas

We want to hear from you! Tell us about any earth friendly activities you may have. If we use them in **Raising An Earth Friendly Child, Level 2**, we will send you a free autographed copy and we will list your name in the acknowledgements.

Send in your ideas as soon as possible. You may write to us c/o the following address:

Debbie Tilsworth
c/o Raven Press
1900 Raven Drive, Suite 101
Fairbanks, Alaska 99709-8358

Thanks! We look forward to hearing from you.

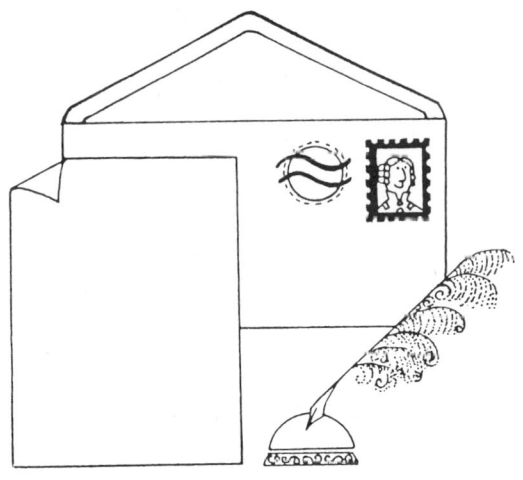

ORDER FORM

Enclosed please find my check for $19.95 plus $3.00 Shipping & Handling to cover the cost of each copy of RAISING AN EARTH FRIENDLY CHILD, Level I, ordered direct from the Publisher (ISBN 0-9627446-7-0). Please rush the book to me at the following address:

Name: _____

Address: _____

_____

City: _____ State: _____ Zip: _____

No. of Copies Ordered: _____

TOTAL Amount Enclosed: _____

Check below if desired:

____ Please add my name to your mailing list and notify me when RAISING AN EARTH FRIENDLY CHILD, Levels II and III become available.

Make checks payable to Raven Press

Order forms should be mailed to:

Raven Press
1900 Raven Drive, Suite 101
Fairbanks, Alaska 99709 8358